BIG LEARNING DATA

By Elliott Masie

With Bob Baker & Learning CONSORTIUM Members
www.biglearningdata.com (for resources and updates)

ASTD
PRESS

ASTD Press is an internationally renowned source of insightful and practical information on workplace learning, performance, and professional development.

ASTD Press
1640 King Street Box 1443
Alexandria, VA 22313-1443 USA

Ordering Information: Books published by ASTD Press can be purchased by visiting ASTD's website at store.astd.org or by calling 800.628.2783 or 703.683.8100.

ISBN-10: 1-56286-909-4
ISBN-13: 978-1-56286-909-0
e-ISBN: 978-1-60728-647-9

ASTD Press Editorial Staff:
Director: Glenn Saltzman
Manager, ASTD Press: Ashley McDonald
Community Manager, Learning Technologies: Justin Brusino
Senior Associate Editor: Heidi Smith
Editorial Assistant: Ashley Slade
Cover Design: Marisa Kelly
Interior Design: Abella Publishing Services
Printed by: Versa Press, East Peoria, IL, www.versapress.com

TABLE OF CONTENTS ▰

DEDICATION

Big data can help create big learning. Let's approach big data as learners, embracing these two perspectives:

The price of light is less than the cost of darkness.

—Arthur C. Nielsen

Not everything that can be counted counts, and not everything that counts can be counted.

—Albert Einstein

FOREWORD

Nate Silver loves data. And he knows how to use it. Silver, who left a job as an economic consultant with KPMG and nurtured his love for statistics and baseball, developed a system for projecting player performance and careers. That system, Player Empirical Comparison and Optimization Test Algorithm (PECOTA), is used by baseball business professionals to predict the performance and value of major league players.

Nate Silver is also the guy who accurately predicted the election outcomes in 49 of 50 states in the 2008 U.S. presidential election, and improved his own stats by accurately predicting the election outcomes in all 50 states in the 2012 election. Data, demographics, behavior—and the correct analysis of all of it—are powerful, and always have been.

But in today's digital landscape, one where people walk around with access to the world's knowledge in their pockets and regularly interact with millions of pieces of information, data takes on new dimensions. We are only beginning to conceptualize what can be done with the mammoth amount of information to which we have access.

I have talked about the power of technology in the learning profession for years. It is revolutionizing the way learning and development practitioners do their work. Leveraging big data is the next logical step in this evolution. The outputs of technology—the data that we gather—provide learning professionals a new vantage point from which to view the work they do.

I am excited about this book that Elliott Masie and his team of collaborators have created. What I found in these pages was a comprehensive SWOT analysis of big data and its implications for the training and development profession. Most refreshing are the honest questions asked by the contributors who wonder whether the field is ready to embrace, understand, and apply the power of big data in their work. The writers identify the strengths and weaknesses, the opportunities and threats that exist as the learning profession gets its collective arms around the what, why, and how of slicing and dicing more information than ever before.

For me, one of the most powerful chapters in the book Is chapter 6, "Stakeholder Perspectives and Needs for Big Learning Data," because it talks about impact, the real heart of the issue. "Analytics and business go hand in hand," the authors say. I believe that learning and business go hand in hand too. Training professionals are wise to make their value proposition to the organization in the language of business. This is something I talked about in depth in *Presenting Learning.* More importantly, for learning to really be the business driver it can be, it is incumbent on training professionals to know and understand the business, who the stakeholders are, and how learning can help those stakeholders achieve their objectives. Big data holds the promise of new insights and of exploring new ways to drive results. It is literally untapped potential at our fingertips.

In Silver's 2012 book, *The Signal and the Noise: Why So Many Predictions Fail but Some Don't,* he states, "The numbers have no way of speaking for themselves. We speak for them. We imbue them with meaning. Like Caesar, we may construe them in self-serving ways that are detached from their objective reality." This is the exact challenge identified and addressed in the book you are now reading.

We have access to volumes of data but we must understand what it can tell us, what it does tell us, and as importantly what it can't and doesn't tell us. As training professionals, we take that information and layer it over the organizational goals we are seeking to support, the gaps we are trying to close, and the engagement and retention metrics we are trying to improve. And then we create courses, programs, initiatives, and processes that have sustained business impact.

Big Learning Data addresses all of this. From explaining why it's important to the field, to identifying impacts on and cautions for practitioners, to offering case studies that frame the discussion, this book is an important and timely work that every learning professional should read. I believe we owe Elliott and his team a debt of gratitude for bringing this book to us at this critical time. Always forward thinking, Elliott is calling attention to the next transformative opportunity for our field.

Big learning data can empower us to develop the knowledge and skills of professionals around the world in ways that we've never been able to do before. It's never been a more exciting time to be in the learning profession.

—Tony Bingham
September 2013

INTRODUCTION

We live in an extraordinary time in history when it comes to the volume of data that exists around us and the volume that is being created. Data are everywhere. Consider this:

* Intel Corporation estimates that the world generates 1 petabyte (1,000 terabytes) of data every 11 seconds, or the equivalent of 13 years of high-definition (HD) video (Finnan, 2013).

* The proliferation of devices such as PCs and smartphones worldwide. Increased Internet access within emerging markets, and the boost in data from machines such as surveillance cameras or smart meters have all contributed to the doubling of the digital universe within the past two years alone. There is now a mammoth 2.8 ZB (zettabytes), according to a December report titled "IDC Digital Universe," which was sponsored by EMC Corp.

This has opened the door to the world of big data. Big data is generated and affects our lives on a daily basis:

* According to a Cisco report in June 2012, big data solutions could help reduce traffic jams or even eliminate them with predictive, real-time analysis on traffic flows. The data could feed immediate changes to traffic signals, digital signs, and routing—before backups begin. Paper receipts from retailers and banks that clutter one's wallet are moving toward replacement by electronic records. Businesses could enrich these records through contextual and comparative information. The report also noted that individuals

could manage, share, monetize, and utilize the data through, for example, budget management and health advice applications.

* As of early 2012, the big data market stood at just more than $5 billion based on related software, hardware, and services revenue, according to market research firm Wikibon. The total big data market reached $11.4 billion in 2012, ahead of Wikibon's 2011 forecast. The big data market is projected to reach $18.1 billion in 2013, an annual growth of 61 percent. This puts it on pace to exceed $47 billion by 2017, the report said.

What is *big data*, exactly? Definitions of big data vary. There are, however, several common characteristics in these definitions. The term generally describes three aspects of data:

* **Volume:** Big learning data enables an organization to access and analyze a volume of data for a richer perspective. *Volume* can mean information about thousands of learners taking a course or experience. *Volume* can mean you are looking at multiple data points, over time, about a single learner. *Volume* can provide data on a deeper and richer set of learning activities—even capturing the time a learner paused while answering a specific question. And, *volume* might someday bring together learning data from hundreds of organizations, providing a global perspective.

* **Velocity:** Big learning data enables learners and organizations to have rapid access to data—even in real time. Imagine a worker entering a wrong answer into an assessment exam. *Velocity* would instantly provide him with remedial and enrichment options based on his historical learning patterns and successful strategies from thousands of other learners who also failed that question. Finally, *velocity* would allow learning producers the ability to make adjustments to content delivery—based on rapid analysis of user experience—on a continual basis.

* **Variety:** Big learning data connects the dots, weaving together a wider variety of information from talent, performance, demographics, and business metrics. You can then see the correlations between learning performance and other behavior and background points. Imagine correlating performance reviews

with learning activities and hiring data, either for thousands of employees or drilled down to a single worker.

And with this have come new methods for working with data: data analytics. These approaches are required to handle the volume of data and to portray them in useful and powerful ways that result in new capabilities or significant improvements in existing ones. Analysis of big data also offers the potential for better predicting the future with *predictive analytics*.

Big Learning Data

So, what does big data mean for our workplace learning field: big learning data?

Quite simply, big learning data is big data that we apply to our learning field. But the implications of big learning data are far from simple. It will require us to think first of all about data in new ways, including why big learning data is important, as well as to develop new skills and mindsets in our field to deal with it. It also requires us to take a deeper look at which data are—and will be—available, not just in our learning functions, but in our organizations and with our learners, for example. At the same time, our organizational stakeholders will play key roles in how we move forward as learning functions with big learning data. The roles that learning leaders might play in leveraging big learning data are also significant.

Big learning data has the potential to play a substantial role in shaping the future of learning from various perspectives. For example, imagine how robust data and analytics might enable us to more deeply personalize the learning experience. Collecting data on the time between keystrokes by the learner might provide insights into how confident she is and may afford the opportunity to design in "enriching" experiences. Plus, big learning data might help us become more effective in an area that has been challenging for learning professionals: learning evaluation. It also has the potential to inform many more strategic decisions about how learning works in our organizations, including what technologies to invest in.

At the same time, there are numerous challenges and traps that we as learning professionals need to watch out for and guard against. Chief among them is the quality and value of the data itself. Some data is just "silly" data. And because there is a lot of it, not all has value or will have impact. We need to be careful about how much we depend on data for making decisions. Lessons of experience teach that over-dependence on quantitative data without qualitative insights can be a trap. We also face challenges in how much data to share and collect. Along with this, there will no doubt be issues of ethics and transparency that will become both significant and problematic.

What You Will Find in This Book

In this book, we bring together multiple perspectives on big learning data for a practical look at what it means and the potential it offers in the world of workplace learning. We explore the topic from the point of view that in our organizations, the process of workforce learning generates an enormous amount of data that ranges from who takes which courses or consumes which learning objects, to the timing and impact of learning activities on performance or career retention, to how many seconds people watch certain videos or access key documents on the corporate server. Data are generated by the actions and decisions of learners, managers, customers, and others. Some of the data are meaningful, some are confusing, and some are intriguing. Assuming we had the learning systems and analysis models, what big learning data would we collect and use to improve the learning process?

The perspectives presented in this book focus on several important aspects of the answer to this important question. The opening chapters from Elliott Masie, Nigel Paine, and Donald H. Taylor present an overview of what big learning data is and why it is important. They foreshadow how the workplace learning field will be affected as big data's influence increases, and how skills and mindsets will need to change. The next chapters by Tom King, Coley O'Brien, Rahul Varma, Dan Bielenberg, Dana Alan Koch, A.D. Detrick, and Elliott Masie provide more in-depth perspectives on key aspects of big learning data, including: sources of data and analytics; the role of learning leaders; how big data can affect learning design in training programs; the relationship with learning function stakeholders; and the potential dangers of big learning data. The book concludes with several case studies from Nickole Hansen, Peggy Parskey, Jennifer O'Brien, Jeff Losey, Ben Morrison, and Doug Armstrong that discuss how their organizations are implementing a big learning data approach. Thought leadership in the education field extends beyond workplace learning, for example, also in the K–12 space. So we have added a summary of the U.S. Department of Education's recent report *Expanding Evidence Approaches for Learning in a Digital World*, which focuses on how big learning data might inform sound decisions, fuel innovation, and optimize technology-based learning resources.

References

EMC Corporation. (2013). *IDC Digital Universe*. Accessed on September 6, 2013 from www.emc.com/leadership/programs/digital-universe.htm.

Finnan, J. (2013). "Big Data Factoids." myCIOview. Accessed on October 3, 2013 from http://mycioview.com/entry/big-data-factoids.

SECTION I

BIG LEARNING DATA AND DATA ANALYSIS ARE IMPORTANT

CHAPTER 1

ON BIG LEARNING DATA

THOUGHTS FROM ELLIOTT MASIE

Elliott Masie

To open this book, we share some perspectives on where we are and where we might be headed with big data in organizational learning. These perspectives are shaped by experience in working with more than 240 public and private sector organizations of various sizes that comprise the MASIE Learning CONSORTIUM.

Big Learning Data

Overall, we see big data as the ability to analyze, compare, and slice enormous streams of data—primarily by-products of the digital age. Therefore, what makes big data "big" is looking at a vast number of data elements across a volume of incidence—not just one person, but thousands of people, for example. It is also the phenomena of now having very large amounts of data from myriad sources: many transactions, computer movements, and aggregations of some noncomputer behaviors, including biological phenomena. However, there is also a lot of meaningless data. As such, part of the big data model is figuring out "Where do I look at a vast volume from a value perspective?"

Big data opens the possibilities of understanding at a deeper level that, in most cases, can't be achieved otherwise. For example, it can give an historical analysis: why did people vote that way at the poll; why did people go or not go to that course? It can also provide a predictive framework: how do I get more people to a course; or get more people to the poll; or even on some level, how do I use a design phenomenon to personalize for an individual experience based on his history and how a wider set of data is used.

Big data in learning provides learning professionals with new opportunities. Whether the learning professionals want to use big data or not, businesses in many cases are already leveraging big data for business intelligence and are inevitably going to draw the connection between learning and customer satisfaction. We believe that what learning folks can do, whether or not their organizations are pushing for business intelligence, is to use these data points to help them better design learning, better evaluate the impact of learning, better fuel an evidence-based approach to experimentation, and better create personalization.

Big learning data will ultimately come down to value. That is, what can we gain from big data? Benefits can be for the learner, the designer, the manager, or the organization, enabling each one to do something better, faster, cheaper, more strategically, and more persuasively.

Sources of Big Learning Data

The problem with data, historically, is that we've always gone for the low-hanging fruit. We, as learning professionals, have collected inexpensive, easily acquired data from people while they are in our domain, usually a classroom or program. In fact, data that may be the most impactful is higher up the tree. For example, it's finding out six weeks after training from a learner's manager whether there was a difference. Or if you go back to the learner a year after the program, or three years later, you can find out whether he is still with the company, or if there was any difference in performance.

We also may need to rethink where we get our data. We will need to look at learning in the broader context, and when we do, we will begin to see many potentially valuable data sources, including many that already exist. One way to look is from a broader human resources perspective. The relationship between selection, training, and competency is very interesting. Often we evaluate the impact of a leadership program, for example, with the assumption that we did great things in the program. In reality, we know that a lot of it has to do with how well we select the people to go into that program from our pool, and how well we select people to join the organization. We might also look at what they did before they came into the program and what their manager did after they left the program. Another way to think about where to get data is in an element of design: the usability of learning content and resources. For example, every instructor will mention books, articles, and now TED Talks, every time they teach. Instructors typically mention them based on their opinions about those they enjoy. We might look at whether people went to them, or if they completed them, what they thought about them, and so on. So if I as an instructor was in a more data-rich environment, those dropped resources in my conversation, or in my e-learning module, or in my WebEx session, would be informed and maybe challenged by what the data puts out there.

We will also need to consider alternative approaches to collecting data, which have some important implications. Some areas where our approaches to data sources might change include:

* **Depth of measurement:** We have looked, for example, at whether learners passed an exam. But more valuable data might include not just the answer, but also characteristics of how learners answer the question—such as, how long it took them to answer and whether their mouse hovered over a wrong answer for a while.

* **Expense:** We have relied on inexpensive data. Some data that we will use in big learning data will be more expensive to get than what we have traditionally used. But what we easily collected tended to be modestly superficial. Collecting data through interviews with managers of learners, for example, costs much more, but yields much more data.

* **Types of data:** We have looked for how learners have answered a question. But more valuable would be their confidence in answering the question.

As an example of these points, early in my career I was involved with The Rockefeller Foundation, and I was funding some arts and education programs. We were trying to evaluate whether people went to see art that we hung in museums. We went through all sorts of ways of doing it and Robert Stake, who was one of the godfathers of evaluation, had a great comment: "What you need to do is buy a carpet-measuring device and roll it around the museum to see where the carpet was mashed down the most." And sure enough, it was a measure of which pieces of art got the most attention, good or bad. Well, nobody would have ever said in a grant to The Rockefeller Foundation that we're going to measure carpet. But in a big data model, we would measure carpet. Are there the equivalent of "carpet data" that we need to ferret out?

Shifts From Big Learning Data

As we move toward big learning data approaches, we will need to shift in the learning field in at least two ways.

1. We need to have an anthropological view of the learning process, to understand that there are many factors that may influence learning. We need to realize learning may influence or may support or destroy the impact of learning, thus broadening our view of potentially relevant data.

2. We need to have an analytical approach, which says that if we gather this data, we need to analyze that data with integrity and with a more sophisticated multivariable analysis. How do we display that data so it brings meaning to people? If I'm given this data, what do I do with it strategically, and how do I handle that?

In making these changes, it will be important to also consider that we want to be anthropologists who are analytical *and* have an ethical code. As we broaden our data and analysis aperture, this will become more important for learning professionals. For example, it would be interesting to ask every person in class what the level of stress in their life outside of work is. It may be the key indicator of success. But we don't know how to ethically ask that question, so while there are data points that may be really powerful, we have to ask if they are within our ethical domain.

Some Challenges Ahead

There will be numerous challenges that learning organizations will confront as they increasingly move toward big learning data. One challenge is readiness—the extent to which individuals making decisions are ready to operate with a massively enhanced set of data. For example, designers pick a few elements that they want, but they aren't limitless in that. At which point do we analyze what color background works best, or at which point do we analyze the font size? And on some level, they may all be key, but I don't know if we have the design skills to do this. It's not emotional intelligence; it's the big data intelligence we need to do this.

A second challenge is the need at some point to upgrade, alter, or change learning systems. Most learning management systems (LMSs) are not big data ready. It doesn't mean that they couldn't be adapted or enhanced, but most of them are not big data ready. Also, there ultimately is an open model of big data in which we understand that data exist in many domains. We need to understand where and how and in what way it's appropriate to share and use that data, because it could lead from a performance or personnel perspective to some pretty radical things happening. For example, if I suddenly realize that the 15 people who left the organization as managers were all hired by Claire, then we don't have a learning problem, we have a Claire problem. So once you take away the boundaries, you're going to end up with some perspectives that aren't in your area of control, and that can be intriguing.

Another challenge is being able to distinguish between valuable and "silly" data. We can have very elaborate analysis of things that are meaningless. For example, we can have an infographic of the total number of people that have gone through training. It's an interesting piece of data and we can get very granular, but we need to take a big data analysis approach to say: who they are; why they went to the training; what the outcome was; what happened to the people who didn't go; or how the outcomes are variable. If we don't analyze it from a big data perspective, then it's lacking something.

Potential Impact

If you posit that big learning data will create an environment of rich informa-tion, it would suggest that the learner will be better informed and it would then allow for greater personalization. For example, say someone wants to take job B, having done job A for a year. Big data would indicate, first of all, the number of people who did A that then got to B. Of the people who got B, what preparation did they have? It would also indicate which learning programs were most effective, and what the timing was for when they attempted to change to job B. It might even get all the way down to if we could do it, and we could sort against the volumes, then we are not just targeting against three people. If it's in a big organization, if it's the federal government, I may be looking across a thousand people who did that. We might find that watching videos and spending three hours with a key manager once a week is more powerful than going away for a 28-day training program, so that the knowledge set could allow the learner to be a designer, a decider, or a targeter.

Big learning data also could be informative from a feedback and con-text arena, because very often somebody might fail at a topic but not know why they are failing. It becomes interesting when the learner can look not just at themselves, but at other people who have had that experi-ence. They may certainly get an insight, either that would explain it so they are not frustrated or that they could use to correct it—so that they could succeed again.

Also, if you implemented big data in a comprehensive way, the learner potentially becomes very invested in inputting data to the process, because they see the impact of how it works. We would need to be concerned about whether learning can be micro-engineered by data, and I am always a combination of a behaviorist and a more gestalt approach. That said, ulti-mately we can program a better mix or selection, though we would want to be cautious if we thought that with enough data we can program every-body to a predicted success at a predictive rate, and at a predictive time, and have very few failures in that process.

Looking Ahead

When looking out some years, the question arises: How different will learning be in organizations that embrace a big learning data approach? We would say moderate, because we in learning organizations are still creatures of habit. A lot of learning is culturally habit-based and because it is so, contrary to most hype, we have never seen an instant revolution in our field. One might say webinars were a brand new invention, but they go back to the mid-1990s when the first webinar providers came out. So there aren't true overnight successes.

We have some decisions to make that will affect the pace of adoption of a big learning data approach. We will need to decide, for example, whether we use big data and in which formats. Do we use it retroactively as analytical to evaluate what worked or did not work at a big level? Do we use it predictively to influence what we do going forward at a big level, or do we take the personalized side of big data where we use the data to target you? In some sense that's the Amazon.com model, which uses a lot of data from a lot of people and then uses the data about what each individual has looked at, thought about, visited, and not bought. And so then we could target an advertisement about other learning opportunities they might need. I don't know whether we call that last bit big data. I think we are too early in the process and some people would say no, because if you are talking about a unit of one it's not big data to them. But you could do that level of personalization if somewhere you had collected big data.

We are in the early stages of considering the possibilities for big learning data in the organizational workplace. And while exciting, this means that we have a lot of work to do as learning professionals. Some early thought leaders are emerging and are beginning to define the dimensions of where big learning data may lead us. My hope for readers of this book is that you will be active learners, evidence-based experimenters, and will explore both the opportunities and challenges that big learning data presents to the learning and knowledge world. Big data is here. Our opportunity is to shape big learning data to help create big—personalized—effective learning for employees and organizations.

CHAPTER 2

WHY ARE BIG LEARNING DATA AND DATA ANALYTICS IMPORTANT?

Nigel Paine

Affecting Performance

Learning leaders are increasingly accountable for proving that what they do adds value and affects business performance. The simple truth is that data starts the conversation about effectiveness. Increasingly, it is harder and harder to have a conversation around the effectiveness and impact of learning in the absence of any hard data. A pile of smile sheets that proves conclusively everyone enjoyed a particular learning experience no longer works. As the quality guru W. Edwards Deming said a long time ago: "In God we trust; all others bring data."

Set this against a world where data-backed research indicates that effective training and development does, indeed, deliver results. The annual *Good Company* review conducted by Laurie Bassey and Associates concludes that companies with high T&D investment outperform the S&P average return by 17 percent. The key word is, however, *effective*. What makes learning effective takes us back to data!

17

So what is big data and what is learning analytics? And how can they be linked to learning effectiveness? Let's start with big data. In the book *Networked*, the authors describe big data this way:

> "Big data is a loosely defined term used to describe data sets so large and complex that they become awkward to work with using standard statistical software. The rise of digital and mobile communication has made the world become more connected, networked, and traceable, and has typically led to the availability of such large data sets" (Rainie and Wellman, 2012).

In other words, there are many new ways of collecting and sorting data in the age of ubiquitous mobile devices, software logs, and wireless data, and these need new ways to analyze that data. Where data are successfully processed and analyzed, there is clear competitive advantage. If you compare a bookshop, with its rudimentary stock control, and Amazon, you can clearly see the advantage. The bookshop has only a small idea of its market and market trends at a very general level. Compare that with Amazon, where every transaction and every move through the Amazon website is tracked against each individual visitor. Amazon gathers massive data sets on purchasing trends, on how much interest particular products or brands generate, and on what an individual enjoys viewing or is curious about without purchasing. The longer the exploration, the greater the interest. The company can therefore suggest things an individual may like—items that other individuals who bought what you're about to buy also bought. It's no secret that Amazon's level of personalization also suggests items to you that you may be interested in, in the future. Which organization draws the most competitive advantage, the bookshop or Amazon? The answer is obvious.

Learning analytics clearly has its roots in research models in general. What is new, however, according to the Athabasca academic George Siemens, is "the rise of quantity and quality of data being captured as learners engage in learning processes. As a consequence, better and more data analytics have gained attention in education." Learning analytics is therefore "the measurement, collection, analysis, and reporting of data about learners and their contexts, for the purpose of understanding and optimizing learning environments in which it occurs" (Society for Learning Analytics Research, 2013). There is also the bigger picture of understanding what needs to meet and what environments to build in the first place.

Businesses are also awash with data. From social networking to intranet access, each key press and each comment, although relatively insignificant on their own, reveals striking trends when gathered and analyzed. This is really important within business and it should be really important within learning.

My first conclusion is that big data is as much a state of mind as a state of information. If you are sensitive to the data all around you, you can begin to set in motion the analytic processes that will yield insight and help your decision making. If you are unaware of the data, you'll miss many opportunities.

Mini Case Study

The T&D team in a company started to take an interest in the sales data being gathered from a combination of customer feedback and social networking comments. Once the team was able to examine the data, they saw the data revealed some strikingly clear insights into skill deficits among the salesforce. The team instituted many performance management solutions (just-in-time small learning bites), as well as two learning courses to up-skill that group. Over a period of six months, the team tracked the same data and could therefore draw some fairly conclusive evidence about the impact of the programs, as well as how they directly affected the bottom line of the company. This process gave the T&D team a huge amount of respect and the increased credibility of the learning function.

Although the team in the case study above had been using big data and the analytical tools used to make sense of it, and refined the T&D programs as a result, they had not gathered any of this data. They had simply made use of what the company was already producing. There are many instances where the learning operation can increase focus and effectiveness simply by engaging with the increasing amounts of data that the rest of the company is using to help its decisions. That can take place before a single dollar has been spent on any specific learning analytics.

As data volume increases from multiple sources, so does the reliability of the data. The real dream that big data holds out is the competitive advantage that the velocity of almost real-time decision making can offer. This can lead to increased agility at both organizational and individual levels. For learning to be able to provide what is required, almost before the individual or the group is aware of that need, is extremely attractive as well as powerful. You could argue that human resources are the last great area where analytics have yet to make a difference. With the increasing availability of data from sensors, software, social networking, and more, it is highly unlikely that this will continue to be the case. That is why IBM, Accenture, Deloitte, and McKinsey are currently taking such an interest in big data.

We have been taught to clear the mud of data from the shiny object of insight. Most of the data that we currently collect are washed away to reveal the golden grains of truth that traditional learning analysis has revealed. In many ways, this process means that training and development is throwing away a huge opportunity to be more accountable, business-aligned, and relevant. This is a prize worth having.

Moving Forward

Getting it right with big data means not focusing on a single stream of information. The real insights come from what Elliott Masie calls "the data weave." We can now combine various data streams and process them as a single element. As the data points increase, the value of those insights increases proportionally. As you move forward on this journey, here are eight key points to consider:

1. **Ask good questions of the learner.** Not "did you enjoy this course," but "would you recommend it to others"!

2. **Do not present spreadsheets as conclusions.** They are your starting points. Take the data and tell their story. Describe what they show and indicate how sure you are of your conclusions.

3. **Great presentations are brief.** State your findings and what you propose to do as a result. The data are there to back up your story, not to be the story itself.

4. **Do not measure everything.** Select what is most important and focus on getting good data for that. Not everything deserves the same degree of attention.

5. **Bear in mind that in most cases "roughly reasonable data"** (a phrase coined by John Mattox, Head of Research at KnowledgeAdvisors, during a workshop in March of 2013) **is perfectly acceptable.** If you state your degree of assurance with the conclusions, either higher or lower depending on the nature of the data, most people will go along with you. It is, in any case, never a good idea to be 100 percent confident of any conclusion!

6. **The key time to sample your results is around one or two months after any learning event.** That sampling should indicate changed behavior and embedded skills. Collecting the same data one day after a program has finished proves nothing about impact, only retention.

7. **What you are doing is using numbers to make better business decisions.** Ask what decisions you are trying to make before you begin that process. The question comes first, and then data help provide the answer. It is easy to use big data to provide answers to questions that no one is interested in. The rest of the business will tell you what the interesting questions are, and what is less interesting.

8. **The training and development team needs to own the story.** They need not own the data, and they need not have done the data processing. They do, however, need to be able to trust that the outcomes indicated are credible and reliable.

My first conclusion was that big data is a state of mind; my second is that big data encourages a more holistic approach to training and development. If you're looking at, for example, a leadership program, you will need the data to tell you where to focus, plus the data to tell you whether the program achieved its aims. Then you need the data to tell you whether your program has made an impact on behavior and improved leadership processes. Some of that information will come through IT systems, but some of it will come through interviewing key staff, program participants, and those who are led by the leaders going through the program. It is that combination of hard and soft data that will enable you to begin to draw some firm conclusions about impact and effectiveness.

All the big consultancies are anxious to provide learning analytics services to companies. They have the tools and knowledge about the processes involved. It is also possible to do it in a different way. Many of the analytics tools are open source; infographic tools are available free or very cheaply from newly established, small companies. There are even single traders or small groups who will take your data and process it on your behalf. You do not have to have data scientists on the payroll to make use of the insights that data scientists can yield.

Conclusions

If you think of a game of darts, everyone has three darts to throw, but not everyone will score 180 each time. You have to recalculate after each throw. Working with big data is similar. The fact that you have not gotten every piece of software, social networking site, or data-gathering instrument working for you, with a team of data scientists to process and analyze that information and turn it into insight and knowledge, does not mean that this area is out of bounds. Everybody can do something. Everybody can begin to understand the processes that are required to make big data and learning analytics work for them. This is both the challenge and the opportunity.

The October 2012 *Harvard Business Review* ended one of its big data articles with the statement "Big data is an epic wave gathering now, starting to crest. If you want to catch it, you need people who can surf" (Davenport and Patil, 2012). This is true, but you also need people who can act on what the data is telling them, and you need people to be data-driven.

References

Davenport, T., and D.J. Patil. (2012). "Data Scientist: The Sexiest Job of the 21st Century." Retrieved September 9, 2013 from http://hbr.org/2012/10/data-scientist-the-sexiest-job-of-the-21st-century/ar/1.

Rainie, L., and B. Wellman. (2012). *Networked: The New Social Operating System.* Cambridge, MA: MIT Press.

Siemens, G. (2013). *Learning and Knowledge Analytics.* Retrieved on January 19, 2013 from www.learninganalytics.net/.

Society for Learning Analytics Research. (2013). "About." Retrieved on September 9, 2013 from www.solaresearch.org/mission/about/.

CHAPTER 3

THE SKILLS AND MINDSET REQUIRED FOR BIG LEARNING DATA

Donald H. Taylor

Big Data Is Here to Stay

Every part of our daily lives now generates data, from our shopping, to our mobile phone use, to our interaction with the Internet. For good or bad, the collection, analysis, and interpretation of this data is now part of the world we live in. Big data is here to stay.

What effect will this have on the training and development (T&D) profession? It is clear that the advent of big data presents us with both opportunities and challenges, but my concern here is not *how* we use that data. It is whether we in T&D are *able* to. With some exceptions, I am largely skeptical that we have the necessary skills, and I believe this represents a major challenge to the profession. As the analysis of data and an understanding of its complexities and meaning come to be an essential part of business life, we run the risk of being excluded from serious dialogue if we are unable to be part of the big data conversation.

T&D Skill Sets

The Learning and Performance Institute's (LPI) free-to-use *Capability Map* describes the 27 skills that make up most of the T&D profession, ranked on a scale of ability of 1–4. Our report on nearly 1,000 self-assessments against the map over its first six months of use reveals some dramatic truths about the profession, and they do not bode well for us as the information manipulators that we will have to be in the future.

Of the 983 individuals who assessed themselves against the map, the greatest number rated themselves against the skills of "presentation delivery" (873) or "face-to-face learning" (738), and they scored themselves highly—an average of 3.26 and 3.36 respectively on a 1–4 scale—making these the two most highly scored skills of the 27 on the map. That is to be expected. As a profession, we are rooted in the tradition of designing materials and of delivering courses.

In contrast, the average score for "data interpretation" was ranked 23rd of the 27 skills, at just 2.36, and only 319 people assessed themselves against it at all. In other words, a small proportion of us believe we have any ability in data interpretation, and even then, we do not consider ourselves very good at it.

The Need For Analytical Skills

This is not a criticism, just a fact: People do not typically enter the T&D profession with analytical skills. They typically join because they are subject matter experts, or because they are good with people or design. You can be those things and *also* have great analytical skills, but most people don't. There are exceptions, of course, and we probably all know T&D people who love to crunch the numbers—for example, in the analyst community—but they stand out precisely because they are exceptions.

If we don't have these skills in large measure already, can they be learned? They can, but not all analytical skills are equally important or equally easy to learn. There are at least two things required in dealing with big data. The first is to find and query the data. The second: to interpret your findings.

The first of these can certainly be learned, and by this I mean the technical skills of running a database query, searching across tables of data to find what you want, and running analysis using a tool such as Excel pivot tables to extract the information you need.

But while it is relatively easy to query and mine data (or at least to learn how to do it), the real trick is to interpret that information and put it to use. This is harder to learn.

The problem with interpreting data is that it requires a good feel for data and numbers as well as a sense of what they mean, usually based on a combination of mathematical knowledge and common sense. In the past, this is not an area we have shone in.

Never mind big data—in the past, T&D has had trouble dealing with small data, like a single number. The much repeated canard that people use only 10 percent of their brains is one example. Dr. Eric Chudler of the University of Washington traces the origins of this myth back to 1935 or earlier. Dr. Chudler points out that you don't have to be (as he is) a brain expert to work this out. A moment's careful thought should make it clear that the myth is extremely unlikely. Not only is 10 percent a suspiciously round number (and so unlikely to have come from any real scientific study), but also the idea that we would waste 90 percent of an organ that uses up something like a fifth of the body's energy seems very unlikely. Finally, there is the killer question: What does it actually mean to "use your brain"? Different types of brain scans show very clearly that much of the brain is active most of the time just keeping the body ticking. It may not be mostly consciously thinking, but it is certainly in use. Vaguely defined terms are usually a clear marker of soft thinking and poor data.

The same concerns extend to another much-repeated myth: the addition of numbers to Dale's Cone of Experience and the creation of the proposition that "people remember 10 percent of what they read and 90 percent of what they do." While this has been brilliantly deconstructed by Dr. Will Thalheimer, again, it should have been impossible for this myth to have gotten started, simply because the numbers are too round to be the result of real scientific inquiry, and the labels too vague; do you measure retention directly after reading, after a period, or when? That wooliness should have set alarm bells ringing, yet both myths are still too often repeated by members of the T&D community.

Both these myths succeeded because they conjoin a number to a valid feeling, based on experience, such as *we could be much smarter with a little effort,* or *I remember more about what I do than what I read.* The numbers seem to add extra weight to this feeling, but examined critically, they are spurious. It is this ability to probe data, to have what I call a "good feel for numbers," which the T&D data analyst needs when interpreting data. It is the difference between taking a number at face value—especially when we are emotionally invested in it—and subjecting it to hard testing.

But interpreting data—rather than querying it—goes beyond simply thinking hard about things. It's important to know what you've got when you find it. In T&D, for example, we have to be careful to isolate the cause of any effect. If we carry out some sales training and then sales increase, does that mean the sales training was effective? Not necessarily. Sales could have been on an upward trend anyway, or some external event such as the launch of a new product may have boosted them. The training may have helped, but it may not have contributed all of the effect.

It's also crucial to be familiar with distributions and averages. Suppose team A's performance is on average less than team B's. Does this mean all performers in A are worse than team B? It does not. There could be a single poor player on team A bringing down their average or a super performer on B bringing theirs up. In fact, it is quite possible that most of team A are better than team B, with just a few outliers shifting the averages.

The issue here is that usually we intuitively consider groups of data as spread along a *normal* distribution, because so often it is. The height or weight of any large population, for example, can be plotted on a bell-shaped normal distribution, where the average will indeed be in the middle of the group. Make the population small enough, though, and that pattern will not necessarily apply, and for some things, it will never apply anyway—like wealth. According to U.S. Senator Bernie Sanders, the six Walmart heirs together own more wealth ($100 billion) than the bottom 40 percent of Americans (PolitiFact.com, 2013). The situation is similar in all developed economies. That is not a bell-shaped curve; it's more likely to be a lognormal distribution, with a few very rich people at one end and a long tail of the rest of us.

We Need To Grow

Data is going to play an increasing part in our working lives. The evidence suggests that we do not yet have either enough specialists to really put it to work for T&D, or a broadly spread enough general knowledge that will enable the majority of practitioners to hold their own in any business conversation using data. If we are not to be sidelined, that has to change. The risk of big data is that rather than putting it to good use because we know what we are doing with it, we become the servants of those who do.

References

Chudler, E. (2012). "Do We Use Only 10% of Our Brains?" Retrieved on September 6, 2013 from http://faculty.washington.edu/chudler/tenper.html.

Learning & Performance Institute. (2013). *The LPI Capability Map*. Retrieved on September 6, 2013 from www.learningandperformanceinstitute.com/capabilitymap.htm.

PolitiFact.com. (2012). "Bernie Sanders Says Walmart Heirs Own More Wealth Than Bottom 40% of Americans." Retrieved on September 6, 2013 from www.politifact.com/truth-o-meter/statements/2012/jul/31/bernie-ssanders-says-walmart-heirs-own-more-wealth-bottom-/.

Thalheimer, W. (2006). "People Remember 10%, 20%,…Oh Really?" Retrieved on September 6, 2013 from www.willatworklearning.com/2006/10/people_remember.html.

SECTION II

IMPACTS ON PEOPLE IN THE LEARNING FIELD

CHAPTER 4

BIG LEARNING DATA AND TRAINING PROGRAMS

START SMALL TO GO BIG AND GO BIG TO GO LONG

Tom King

Big data doesn't absolutely require use of seemingly obscure terms and technologies like Hadoop, Storm, and Hunk. Likewise the *thinking* and approaches of big data don't absolutely require thousands or millions of course completions. Big data thinking and approaches can be incredibly useful throughout the full life cycle of training programs. I find it particularly interesting to apply big data principles to both the earliest and latest phases of the course maturity life cycle.

Analytics are typically evaluated after the pilot test of a course and shortly thereafter. If you are lucky, they also get reviewed midway through a course's lifespan, at which point a significant number of employees are in the field applying the coursework, and there's typically no budget for revisions. Often overlooked is the initial inception of training, when big data *approaches* can be most innovative and informative to course *design* (versus course mending or maintenance). Big data approaches can help determine needs, refine designs, and even generate content—long before the final course is delivered or the knowledge and skills go live in the field.

At the other end of the life cycle, courses addressing stable and long-term content can also be neglected. Such courses offer surprisingly rich opportunities for improvement through big data for many reasons beyond the obvious plethora of sample points they can offer relative to a short-lived training offering. In many cases, the audience, context, and relevance of a seemingly stable course can dramatically shift over time and go largely undetected.

I'd like to offer some strategies to apply big data approaches to nascent, emerging courses and mature, stable (or seemingly stable) courses. Let's take a look at using key elements of big data approaches along with "lean startup" tactics when a course is first conceived. Then I'll follow up with big data planning and retrospective approaches for our "old growth" courses.

Start Small to Go Big

I've found *lean startup* to be a valuable tool to use while prototyping learning innovations or developing brand new courses. The *lean startup* is an approach that Eric Ries refined for developing products or services and described in his book *The Lean Startup: How Today's Entrepreneurs Use Continuous Innovation to Create Radically Successful Businesses.* This approach significantly leverages ideas from lean manufacturing, discovery-driven planning, and Steven G. Blank's customer development process (*The Four Steps to Epiphany*). The approach also capitalizes on agile software development approaches, open source software, and easily deployed analytics. Many of these approaches can be used for a rapid-iteration, data-fed approach to instructional design and development.

A better understanding of lean startup will help as we bridge into the topic of big data approaches applied on a small scale during development. Two critical components of lean startup are *actionable metrics* and *split testing*, both of which can pivot toward big data in the long run, while being immediately useful during the near-term, formative stages of course development.

Actionable Metrics vs. Vanity Metrics

Actionable metrics are defined in contrast to *vanity metrics*. In the business of learning, online-student-seat hours might be considered a vanity metric;

it serves up a large number that may paint a rosy picture, but provides little or no actionable information about the course, its outcomes, or its market.

In contrast, an *actionable metric* providing the ratio of course completions to course enrollments might tell us there is a high rate of abandonment, and could lead us to investigation and action. Is this abandonment indicative of bad materials, or perhaps good material that goes on too long? Do students "fail," or do they achieve adequate mastery before completion and just move on?

In a big data world, one might be able to look at the job performance or other metrics and make comparisons between groups that never enrolled, groups that enrolled and completed, and groups that enrolled and abandoned. Significant differences (or lack of significant differences) could tell you a lot about this course.

Imagine if those group differences were available before the design phase or early in the design phase of this course. Going forward, as you start considering a course development effort, you should think about actionable metrics and how early you can even get a small sample.

TIP: First ask yourself, what are my most significant or most risky design assumptions? What actionable metric can I create that would confirm or invalidate each assumption? Then ask, what vanity metrics am I collecting? Can I ignore or even eliminate such metrics and distractions?

Split Testing

Experiments are a way for course designers and developers to learn. A *split test* (also called an A/B Test) is one way to experiment with designs to learn if there are differences in appeal, retention, or ability to apply information. Typically this is done by delivering different learning material nearly simultaneously to different learners and then comparing measurable outcomes.

Organizations are often reluctant to offer two versions of content within a single course for various reasons, including concerns about consistency, compliance, or labor council considerations. Two approaches can help address some of these concerns: early testing of a small amount of content with a broader and larger audience (I call this *design testing*); or what I call *piggybacking*, which is a method where one uses a small amount of content, but with a significantly smaller *and* significantly more representative target audience.

Design testing is a useful way to address concerns about contaminating outcomes of a population by delivering two different versions of the full course. Design testing isn't about the whole course, but is instead about a small element, and it is conducted while in the design phase. For example, you could test a small segment or nano-component with a broad approximation of the target audience. Ideally, we then fully inform the participants of their roles, our goals, and the potential impact or value.

The big data approach of running many, many iterations of a small test can be adapted and applied early in the instructional systems design (ISD) process to validate a key objective, interaction, or educational measurement. Using only a small segment or component can help reduce potential stakeholder concerns—as all of the ultimate target audience will receive a course that implements the full final design. Using a larger, broader audience can help address concerns about the sample size and predictions.

Piggybacking is similar to design testing in that it uses a small segment of the course, but differs in that the material is embedded into or "piggybacks" on an existing course with the same target audience. In this case we trade sample size for fidelity to the target audience. Piggybacking might be done in a formal way, by adding a small amount of time within a course (perhaps at a single interval or a logical break point). In most cases, the material needs to clearly indicate to the learner that this is a nonjeopardy situation; however, their participation and feedback will directly influence future training delivered to them. This is often surprisingly effective at getting useful quantitative and candid qualitative data.

In some cases, the content, activity, or design can be grafted directly into the course unannounced. This might be the case if it is significantly related to the host course, and it is reasonable to expect it will have no adverse impact. You could compare this to how an entrance exam can include extra questions with responses that are recorded, but not scored. Such questions can be correlated with "known good questions" and outcomes, and eventually promoted to active questions in this or another exam. Similarly, our relevant design, activity, or content could be tested and ultimately promoted to production.

TIP: Design a course with reserve capacity to accommodate embedded split testing of course content or piggyback testing of other content. Reserve capacity also provides room to grow, swap, or adjust content as the course matures and additional data offer new insights. Also, early in your design analysis, you should develop profiles for surrogate and extended audiences. Consider what larger groups you can reach out to in order to validate, iterate, and improve design.

Lean Canvas—Getting to a Design That Works

To provide structure around my prototyping and validation efforts, I use a *lean canvas* derived from the framework described by Ash Maurya in *Running Lean: Iterate From Plan A to a Plan That Works*. A sample lean canvas appears in Figure 1.

Figure 1: A SAMPLE LEAN CANVAS WORKSHEET FOR THE LEAN CANVAS WEB SERVICE

Problem	Solution	Unique Value Proposition	Unfair Advantage	• Customer Segments
• Business Models need to be more portable.	Lean Canvas Progress Dashboard Sharing Learning	• Helps startups raise their odds of success.		• Startup Founders (Creators)
• Measuring progress is hard work.		• High level concept:		• Advisors/Investors (Collaborators)
• Communicating learning is critical.	**Key Metrics**	• Gifthub meets WeightWatchers for business models.	**Channels**	• Early Adopter: • Familiarity with Lean Startups, Customer Development, Business Model Canvas
• Existing alternatives: intution, business plan, spreadsheets.		• Startup report card.		

Cost Structure	Revenue Streams

Lean Canvas is adapted from *The Business Model Canvas* (www.businessmodelgeneration.com) and is licensed under the Creative Commons Attribution.

It should be relatively clear to most training professionals that they can map or adjust the lean canvas model for their instructional design and business models by changing "customer segments" to "audience," inserting learning or performance metrics as "key metrics," and so forth. Thus I will leave that as a challenge for the reader to complete.

Perhaps less obvious is that each element entered into the categories of the canvas represents at least one testable hypothesis, and behind each hypothesis there needs to be a test or metric to evaluate. For example, under "problem" we find, "measuring progress is hard work." This must be tested and validated, and the audience should be tested as well (in this case, the "customer segments," including "start-up founders" and "advisors/investors").

To validate the key assumptions and attributes of the problem, you must validate that measuring progress is considered hard work. Likewise, you must validate that you have identified the correct audience subgroups ("customer segments") with testing.

The record of the assumptions, the hypothesis, and the testing/metrics provides us with structure, fluidity, and documentation. It can also be a road map outward to the big data sources that will ultimately refine our solution by proving or disproving assumptions. (It is common for any lean canvas worksheet to have a few assumptions invalidated or iterated over the life of a project.)

Use of the lean canvas can act as a road map for potential big data sources by refining the categories of data and isolating the hypothesis to a small statement that can be validated. Ironically, this narrowing can expand the opportunity for data sources by clarifying the independent variable and reducing the independent variables.

For example, separate activities can be done to validate the problem and to validate the audience groups. This provides benefits at both ends of the spectrum, by either focusing on connecting disparate data sources and reducing down to the key factors (big data), or by starting small and running little experiments to generate just enough data to test a small hypothesis. In this way, your canvas can become a road map for the data elements and schema desired to validate the course, content, media, and outcomes.

While initially developed as a design document, your canvas becomes a structured collection of historical assumptions, hypotheses, tests, and metrics. This is both an incredibly valuable design artifact and a living document that points the way to sustainable courses. In some cases, the tests and canvas can even generate or supersede the course (see sidebar *Lean Canvas, Crowdsourcing, and Data Combine to Usurp a Course*).

Lean Canvas, Crowdsourcing, and Data Combine to Usurp a Course

Imagine a situation, such as utility workers in remote areas, where a distributed group of technicians must receive approximately two days of training on a critical, but seldom-encountered scenario.

Because of the limited availability of subject matter expertise and its distributed nature, the design team chose to create a course outline on a wiki and solicit input from a small group of subject matter experts (SMEs). Small surveys and questionnaires were sent to SMEs to answer based on the wiki content, as a way to validate or disconfirm assumptions about the course outline (topics, hierarchy, and sequence).

Given a valid sequence, the team identified content-specific SMEs. They then validated those selections (assumptions) with the larger group of SMEs, and solicited recommendations for alternative internal and external SMEs. The approved SMEs then contributed a small amount of content to the wiki. The design team had the content validated by the alternative SMEs.

In parallel to these efforts with SMEs, the target audience, the performance metrics, and other lean canvas elements were iterated. Assumptions and metrics were defined, refined, and validated. Throughout the effort, wiki data and web analytics helped support the framework and the validation. Business system data helped confirm events, criticality, audience, and content information.

Eventually, the wiki was opened up as a rich and thorough course document to a segment of the target audience. This audience reacted well and helped further refine the wiki. Several of them suggested they didn't need a course; they just needed the wiki. Several key SMEs concurred. Ah ha! A new assumption to validate: A course isn't needed; the wiki will suffice.

Ultimately, a performance-based assessment determined that the wiki was in fact sufficient. No traditional course was developed. The developers went on to develop other courses, while continuing to have the SME/learner activity, business systems, and web analytics generate data.

Go Big to Go Long

New and old courses both warrant attention. Big data may initially seem like a quick, easy path for determining necessary revisions and setting priorities for course development or maintenance. While it may not be that simple, there are promising opportunities that can be seized with time and some effort. Time itself may be one of those keys.

Rapidly generating large data samples can be a challenge for corporate learning for many reasons, including delivery methods, audience size, and overall course duration (for example, a 30-90 minute online compliance "course"). Large organizations have had significant LMS implementations for 10 or more years. However, many LMS implementations started as department or line-of-business implementations and migrated toward enterprise systems. Furthermore, the vendor landscape has undergone multiple generations of transfers, integrations, mergers, and acquisitions.

As a result of multiple migrations, integrations, consolidations, and transfers, the learner performance data is often reduced to the barest essentials. While we started out collecting more data than we thought we could ever use, we may find that now, all that remains in the LMS as historical data of early courses is basic roster and completion data. Perhaps big data approaches can help with this in the near term, and inform us as we look to securing the future of our learning data in the long term. Commonly, our oldest and seemingly most stable courses may need the most attention, but there is a scarcity of data to justify investment. The question is how to reasonably gather and process data to create actionable information to make intelligent decisions.

Disparate Data Is Big Data

One key facet of big data is leveraging disparate data sources to form a more complete picture. Since we may not have the full original data, big data approaches can lend a hand toward painting a fuller picture of our historical courses and their impacts.

Focusing only on classic structured data will only constrain your potential sources. Look beyond the delivery systems and consider sources like: contracts, design documents, emails, supplier documents, feedback forms, help desk requests, intranet website hits, proxy logs, and more. Think about how the training impact might reveal itself: Could you compare the performance of a new hire before and after training? Obviously, with any indirect comparison, there will be challenges and potentially confounding factors, but comparing different geographies, organizations, time zones, seasons, seniorities, and other demographic factors can help refine the correlations.

By reaching out to disparate big data type sources, you can make more informed decisions about retiring or revitalizing tenured courses. Often these courses are foundational and some people can be reluctant to change them for political or historical reasons. For many of the same reasons, revision, replacement, or removal can have a tremendous positive impact—provided there is an informed rationale for action. Using these approaches, we can ensure appropriate longevity as we strive to make courses "go long."

TIP: Treat your data search like a lightweight version of a course redesign. Look not only at the expected impacts, but also at the underlying assumptions. There is often rich pay dirt to be mined in original project definition, justification, budget, and design documents.

Have the assumptions changed? Are the task analysis and audience analysis still valid? What alternate data sources might exist now for either of those items, and how could they be used in comparison to historical data? Consider how you might adjust the current data collection or create a small experiment using course materials and get that out to a wider audience very rapidly.

The beginning of this chapter introduces lean startup principles and lean canvas as a way to start small with big data concepts. Once we've started small and isolated the known most critical items to track, we can start to go bigger by going long—collecting that data over time for recurring, iterative validation, and refinement based on data.

Patience, Persistence, and Consistency

In many cases, getting a statistically significant sample size requires many, many deliveries of a course. As stakes increase, it becomes more important to strive for statistical significance. Given a limited number of annual, semiannual, or quarterly course offerings, it will take time to get an adequate number of samples. Therefore, it is also important to collect data consistently and to collect it in a way that always allows all data from previous sessions to persist—even if participants must repeat the course due to compliance or other requirements.

Consistency is an obvious consideration, and many references on big data will discuss data consistency and normalization, often citing an example like dates, that can be readily represented in two dozen formats. LMS standards have helped consistency in many ways, but also have created challenges, too.

Data consistency challenges can arise from well-intended flexibility in standards (for example, many AICC systems once accepted "c," "completed," "complete" as synonymous values and many also behaved the same when receiving completion values of "p," "pass," or "passed." ADL SCORM used similar data elements with a slightly different vocabulary, and it too changed from SCORM 1.2 to SCORM 2004. Flexibility in specifications and vendor-specific features lead data formats to diverge.

While convenient in some cases, the changes and leeway in standard specifications also create confusion. As a result, much historical data will need to be normalized. This can be unfortunately complex when crossing standard specifications or releases, or crossing LMS software versions, or crossing epochs in which your organization transitioned from one LMS vendor to another. In such cases, the normalization process may need to cross-reference data to known dates when such transitions occurred, and normalize the data accordingly.

The persistency of data is crucial. Among the lessons learned from retrospective approaches is the value of data logging, or an audit trail. Imagine a situation in which learners must take yearly compliance training online as part of a larger instructor-led course. It would be all too easy to collect demographic data as part of learners' registering into the course, and update their central online profile accordingly. However, this may mean that their job role, rating, or rank is overwritten with each update. When running historical reports, this may mean it always displays a learner's current role or rating, even for a course taken years ago. In such cases, it becomes very difficult to do meaningful comparisons of progression against role or larger comparisons of the post-training performance for a given role.

An audit trail, or persistent snapshots of data, is critical for historical comparisons. For any given report on a course, the learner(s) profile(s) must accurately align with the training record. Such an audit trail will also provide useful way points for future mappings of data in the event vocabularies or data elements change.

Patience is a virtue with big data for learning. There's much talk about big data and the massive amounts of data generated by social media, financial transactions, global positioning devices, video, and the Internet. However, the reality of corporate e-learning is different from the promise of MOOCs and high-volume consumer systems like web searches. Enterprise learning generates significantly lower volumes of recorded or monitored transactions, often with fewer data points per transaction. To paraphrase an advertisement, "We collect data the old fashioned way; we earn it (over time)."

A high stakes regulatory environment can provide us an example of the value of collecting data consistently and over time. It might also remind us that the T&D industry may use big data approaches, but we aren't generally working at the scale of big data (see sidebar *FAA AQP*).

Big Data or Big Data Approaches

Given the available data generators and sources, one might conclude T&D is more suitable to using big data approaches than using the commonly understood big data scope or volume. While some big data systems and tactics won't scale down, many will allow us to scale up the information we use for decisions. Small data can require big judgment. Using big data approaches is one way to collect signals that can improve the big judgments that need to be made for learning and training. Going big in this way can also help us go long, offering a better course for a longer time.

FAA AQP

The U.S. Federal Aviation Administration (FAA) offers an alternative to the traditional means of meeting regulatory training requirements, called the Advanced Qualification Program (AQP). This program has multiple components, but key components include a systematic front-end analysis and a feedback loop for refining training based on data; data about the performance of the course and the pilot's skills, knowledge, and observed performance. A similar program exists in Europe under the European Aviation Safety Agency (EASA), where it is called Alternative Training and Qualification Program (ATQP).

The roots of these programs are in the mid-to-late 1980s, and the FAA program first became available in the early 1990s. While AQP strives to encourage innovation, it also emphasizes the need to "achieve the highest possible standard of individual and crew performance." Quality Assurance (QA) data are critical to obtaining FAA approval for an AQP program and for continuing operations with AQP. There are many important details in the five phases of AQP and the full set of requirements that cannot be adequately be presented here. Suffice it to say that the FAA and the airlines are all highly focused and highly motivated to make sure training supports safe operations.

The relevance of these programs comes when we look at the time and data volume. Once initially available, airlines found that it took three to four years to get to AQP phase IV: initial operations. Throughout the larger process, the QA and data collection is fed back into the program to maintain the approved procedures, standards, and documents. Participating airlines must submit data each month and provide an annual AQP report. The report format specifies 27 data elements per measured item.

It is worth noting that even a top-tier carrier with more than 10,000 pilots would be unlikely to generate a monthly AQP submission report over 5-8MB—a data set small enough to transfer by email. Even with generous rounding, this would be one-tenth of 1GB per year, far from the domain of typical big data exemplars.

The observed time frames are also of interest. While regulatory and airline innovations have reduced the implementation time by half, data collection still takes time. Carriers often collect three to four years of data before making profound changes to an AQP program. Coupled with the time to get through the initial operations phase, this means a six to eight year cycle time—clearly going *long* by any definition of "Internet time."

References

Blank, S.G. (2005). *The Four Steps to the Epiphany: Successful Strategies for Products That Win*. Self-published.

FAA. (2006). *Advisory Circular 120-54A*. Retrieved September 10, 2013 from www.faa.gov /training_testing/training/aqp/library.

Maurya, A. (2012). *Running Lean: Iterate From Plan A to a Plan That Works*. Sebastopol, CA: O'Reilly.

McGrath, R.G., and I.C. MacMillan. (1995). "Discovery Driven Planning." *Harvard Business Review*. Retrieved September 10, 2013 from http://hbr.org/1995/07/discovery -driven-planning/.

Ries, E. (2011). *The Lean Startup: How Today's Entrepreneurs Use Continuous Innovation to Create Radically Successful Businesses*. New York: Crown Publishing.

CHAPTER 5

BIG LEARNING DATA

THREE ROLES OF THE LEARNING LEADER

Coley O'Brien

What's My Role?

As a learning leader, I'm not a measurement expert, data analyst, or "quant jock" (which happens to be a new favorite workplace term that a colleague recently introduced me to). I can build my own pivot table and I know what SQL stands for—which makes me just dangerous enough to know the possibilities when it comes to working with big data.

I enjoy the idea of integrating and connecting large data sets to identify new insights, trends, and meaning. Throughout my career, I've played numerous roles when it comes to working with big data to support workplace learning, including:

* **Builder** = Built spreadsheets and databases for capturing large data sets.

* **Integrator** = Worked with IT and vendors to integrate learning and HRIS systems to generate large data sets.

* **Analyzer** = Helped analyze large data sets to interpret meaning.

Today, the roles required to capture and work with big data are incredibly advanced. Technical experts are working with far more advanced tool sets. The sources for capturing data are growing exponentially. The demands for real-time data are relentless from all levels within organizations.

While data sets, analysis tools, and technical expertise continue to advance, the ability to leverage big data in a strategic and meaningful way for the organization is still a challenge. As I work with people across multiple functions and talk with colleagues from other organizations, I see different challenges within organizations:

* Certain functions within the organization may be "data rich," but don't have the resources, access, or expertise to fully leverage the data.

* Functions may have the right experts or tools, but can't get access to the data.

* Functions may not have full visibility of which data already exist, and could be driving duplicative work.

* Functions may have access to data from other parts of the business, but don't have proper insight in terms of what the metrics really say.

These challenges can lead to numerous frustrations that can ultimately prohibit us from fully capitalizing on the data and insights available to us. To help break through these challenges, I believe there are three key roles that aren't necessarily technical in nature, but are critical to supporting and optimizing big data efforts. These are the roles of connector, catalyst, and context expert. Let me define each of the 3 "C" roles further.

Connector

The *connector* is someone who knows which data are available in organizations, has some basic understanding of what data tell us, and can provide recommendations as to how to best use data to solve real business problems.

Have you ever been in a meeting where someone says, "If we only had data on X, we could do Y," and then someone else in the meeting explains that data already exist and are being captured on a regular basis somewhere else in the organization?

I've been part of this situation many times. Recently, I was in a meeting where someone from marketing expressed interest in having access to data around key operational metrics. I informed them the data already existed and they could easily get access to this data by leveraging existing reporting from our enterprise data warehouse. In this example, I was connecting someone with a business need to another part of the business, where relevant data was already being captured unbeknownst to them. This accelerated their ability to address the business need faster, while likely avoiding some duplicative efforts.

Catalyst

The *catalyst* is someone who knows which groups or individuals control the data and knows how to break through bureaucracies to help others get access to the right data. My experience is that functional groups can be pretty protective of certain data and may be reluctant to share for various reasons. Oftentimes, the concern is that they don't know the group or individual that is requesting the data; they aren't clear on the purpose for accessing the data; and they are concerned what will happen with the data or how it will be interpreted once access is provided.

In these situations, I've been able to help broker "data deals" by helping effectively position the person requesting the data, and clarifying why and how it will be used. For example, I had a conversation with someone who wanted access to specific customer feedback on a certain product. They knew this data existed, but they didn't know who controlled the data and had no concept of how the data was captured. I was able to quickly assess what their need was, then reach out to the owner of the data to explain the request and help facilitate the process. Within hours, the individual had access to hundreds of data points that allowed them to quickly respond to their business issue.

Acting as a catalyst, I was able to help the individual avoid what would have likely been a long and drawn out email exchange and series of approval requests that may have taken weeks.

Context Expert

The *context expert* is someone who has broad knowledge of business metrics and can provide guidance to analysts on key questions, such as:

* What are the desired targets?
* What are acceptable ranges? What's really good? What's really bad?
* With what frequency is the data captured?
* How important is the data viewed by the business? (For example, is it truly a KPI?)
* Who uses this data and how?
* How is this data most easily interpreted by others?

For example, I've been part of cross-functional teams where analysts have access to all the necessary data, but have no idea what "good" or "bad" parameters might be for a particular metric. They were looking to identify outliers, but didn't understand where to establish the proper limits.

Alternatively, a context expert can provide guidance on how to best position or report on data for different audiences. For example, I've worked with analysts that have conducted great analysis and have generated some great charts, which unfortunately would be completely lost on certain audiences. I was able to help provide context as to how these audiences really talked and thought about this type of data, enabling the presenter to modify the charts to provide clarity and greater meaning to the intended audience.

Summary

You're not likely to find people in your organization with clear titles such as connector, catalyst, or context expert. Nor will you likely find people on projects assigned to these specific roles. However, you likely know who some of these people are. As you work on big data projects, think about who in the organization can help you in these areas and then ensure that you're engaging them as part of your process. They will likely help you work faster, more efficiently, and generate a better output.

CHAPTER 6

STAKEHOLDER PERSPECTIVES AND NEEDS FOR BIG LEARNING DATA

Rahul Varma, Dan Bielenberg, Dana Alan Koch

Unexplored Insight

Analytics and business go hand in hand. We analyze data not only to streamline and improve a wide range of processes, but also to learn about the ways our people do business: why they take certain routes to complete their jobs; how they do them; and what they are looking for. This is why big learning data is crucial in the business marketplace. The ability to collect, analyze, and use larger data sets will enable us to learn more about both the direction we're going and the direction we need to go, and allow for the application of that data in the learning space. Unlike traditional analytics, big learning data is immediate data, not past data. It's information that we have not explored: insights we've not yet seen.

A Growing Appetite

At Accenture, we have more than 260,000 people working around the world, represented by various learning stakeholders: business and HR leaders, program sponsors, development teams, faculty, and learners themselves. For our fiscal year 2012, we spent more than $850 million on training, which you could say represents an enormous amount of data. These stakeholders spent a collective 208,900 days in classroom training (that's 52 hours per person) in more than 300 of our training venues worldwide. In the fiscal year 2012 alone, we tracked that close to 7,900 skills had been acquired through our courses—a result of our internal training portal being accessed more than 800,000 times per month. This data is important because these stakeholders are constantly sharing their perspectives on how data enables them to learn what's working for their organizations and what isn't.

That appetite for data and insight to consistently improve our programs seems to only be met with the capabilities big data can now bring us. Most often, for learning analytics projects, the transactional attendance data is easily obtained. Some of the challenges, however, are: the completeness of the data; the curriculum and competency-mapping; the availability of cost data at an instance level; and the total understanding of big learning data. In the learning field, we can take hints from global retailers that have been using big data analytics for years. Retailers use it to better understand the spending habits and decision-making processes and behaviors of their customers, and it helps them improve business operations, focus marketing efforts, increase profits, and remain competitive.

Understanding Stakeholders and Their Needs

With the volume and velocity of learning data increasing, there will be a significant amount of "digital data noise" generated. One filter to help reveal which data are and which data are not important is to have a clear understanding of the learning stakeholders mentioned previously. While several stakeholders are easily identified—business and HR leaders, program sponsors, development teams, faculty, and learners—there are others who may not be as obvious, but would be important consumers of big learning data. As part of a MASIE-sponsored event on the topic of big learning data held in February 2013, an Accenture team led 50 learning professionals through a stakeholder-mapping exercise. This exercise helped us gather a complete listing of stakeholders by visualizing and understanding the interactions, relationships, and mindsets of people who would be involved in or affected by big learning data.

A key dimension was having participants use sticky notes to identify stakeholders and provide a thought or question this stakeholder may have about big learning data. It became clear there is an intricate web of stakeholders who have different, and sometimes overlapping, interests.

Figure 2: STICKY NOTE STAKEHOLDER EXAMPLES

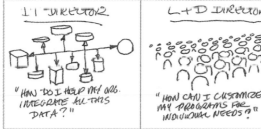

IT DIRECTOR	L&D DIRECTOR	CEO
"How do I help my org integrate all this data?"	"How can I customize my programs for individual needs?	"What value does our learning and information add to company performance?"

Here is more of a sampling of what was identified in the exercise:

Figure 3: STAKEHOLDERS AND RELATED THOUGHTS

Stakeholder	Thought
Human Resources	How can big learning data help with retention and succession planning?
Legal/Compliance	Does collection of data violate any privacy policies?
Training & Development	What will help ensure the right people are getting the right training at the right time? What cultural characteristics affect learning and performance?
Senior Leadership	How can we ensure that learning is making our organization nimble and agile?
Data Scientist	What information has my organization been overlooking? What is the effectiveness of our information landscape?
Prospective Employee	Does the company's use of big learning data help me progress in my career?

The stakeholder-mapping activity not only opened our eyes to the wide range of stakeholders, but it also demonstrated that stakeholders need to understand big data as it relates to learning, so we can continue to improve our business effectively. Chief Learning Officers, for example, must show and understand the return-on-investment. Training and development teams must continually adjust their programs and deliver exactly what is needed, when and where it is needed, and be able to look ahead to tomorrow's demand. We must benefit learners by offering general and specialized training relevant to learners' roles, clients, and industry—as well as their careers—while offering accessible and tailored content to different learning styles.

In many companies, and definitely in learning and IT organizations, the number of stakeholder groups is being expanded to include new perspectives. For a future that includes big learning data, new stakeholders will include data scientists and data visualization specialists. Data scientists will bring new ways of harvesting the high volumes of data. They will help other stakeholders see the power of the information and insight made possible by big learning data. Data visualization specialists will help communicate complex information in understandable ways. We may work with different groups within HR and IT, and may need to raise initiatives up to higher levels so the organization's leadership recognizes clearly the impact of big data in planning for the future.

To do this, there are questions that learning leaders need to address: Which are the most impactful courses or programs? How does it affect the business outcome? Are the right people going for the right programs? How do I anticipate demand and invest in the right areas to maximize the business impact?

To answer these questions, we are using big data to analyze and design our learning strategy, and we expect to see the most impact in three areas:

* **Training Programs**—We can better understand the quality and effectiveness of our training programs, and we will be able to adjust them more efficiently. The ability to analyze and understand huge amounts of data improves our ability to engage learners in meaningful learning experiences. We then can understand what types of activities and which content-delivery approaches are working well and which are not. We now have more precise information on learner preferences, such as delivery methods and content length and presentation, and can be more agile in making changes and improvements.

+ **Skill Development**—Using big learning data will enable us to better predict skills needed in the marketplace and identify what types of capability development will help our employees get those skills quickly. We will be better able to guide our employees to the best resources for learning through sophisticated, data-driven recommendation engines. We will also have insight on global differences in the skills needed and in preferred learning styles. We can tailor training to differences in learning between regions, industries, levels, and workforces.

* **Business Results**—More precisely understanding the skill demands of our business helps us get ahead of the training needs we will have tomorrow and make sure we have not only what clients need but also what they will soon need. In being more proactive in skill development, a company can better identify high-performing individuals and focus on leadership development opportunities, extended training, and succession planning. The data available today makes it easier to match employees with roles—and the training they need—to leverage their strengths and drive business impact.

Influencing a Broader Set of Stakeholders

In addition to using big learning data to train and develop your current workforce, big learning data can also change your company's recruiting strategy and process, as well as the effectiveness of acquiring talent all over the world. Therefore, talent acquisition leaders will be important stakeholders in big data. Successful recruiting organizations that are creating the workforces companies need in the near and long term must be able to integrate big data when looking for certain skill sets, matching talents with roles, and determining where the future talent pool will be for their organizations. Big learning data can help uncover key underlying patterns or establish the cause-effect relationships of a workforce. For example, big data will allow a company to identify training courses that help a certain segment of people develop the right capabilities which manifest through the success of projects, programs, and business.

Overall, big learning data allows us to be much more proactive in equipping people with the skills they need to be competitive in the marketplace.

It provides tremendous insights and knowledge and also requires our organizations to change and adapt, to work with broader teams, to include different perspectives, to envision training in a new way, and to stretch our definitions of learning. Companies that embrace big data in training and learning can better predict the impact training has and will have on their business, as well as predict the skills their employees need today and in the future. This knowledge and insight can transform the way we design, deliver, receive, and evaluate learning programs, and can make learning more effective, relevant, and interesting.

CHAPTER 7

AVOIDING THE DANGERS OF BIG LEARNING DATA

A.D. Detrick

Where is the wisdom we have lost in knowledge?
Where is the knowledge we have lost in information?

—T. S. Eliot

The most obvious benefit of data mining is that extremely large, extremely rich data sets will not only offer insight into what people have learned, but also into how they perform on the job, what behaviors yield the most impact, and even how best to insert learning into their personal landscape. We will be able to uncover activities and trends as they occur, and we will be able to reinforce good learner behaviors and avoid common learner mistakes—almost in real time. Just like with real mining, the more mines we explore, the more gems we hope to uncover. But mines can be dangerous places, prone to structural collapse if not properly designed. And barren mines can be expensive and frustrating. Data mining is no different. Too often, new entrants to the big data environment eagerly jump into data mining with an incomplete understanding of the process and unrealistic expectations of what data mining can—and should—yield. As a result, they end up with an abundance of data that seems to lack any meaningful results that might lead to productive actions. Big data environments created without proper planning or expectation will provide, as T.S. Eliot indicated, lots of information without knowledge and lots of knowledge without wisdom. What follows in this section is a list of the four most common myths and misconceptions of what a big data environment can and should do.

Mistake #1: Deferring Completely to Digital Data in Decision Making

In 2009, Google's top visual designer, Douglas Bowman, exited the company with a blog post that detailed many of his frustrations working in a data-driven environment. By the time he had joined Google, they had been in business seven years without a visual designer, and their decision-making processes were already in place. While Bowman understood the importance of user-response data in driving Google's visual design, he eventually chose to leave over the reach of that data, and how severely it crippled his autonomy as a designer. Even simple judgments that a visual designer could make based on years of experience were subject to test-case analysis. In Bowman's blog post detailing the reasons for his departure, he described a scenario where a design team could not decide between two shades of blue, so they ran quantitative analyses on 41 shades of blue to identify which "performed better." The well-earned autonomy that normally comes with experience and wisdom had been replaced by a data-driven environment, and in doing so, had unwittingly robbed itself of a wellspring of equally rich data.

When we create a big data environment, we too often get mesmerized by the size and scope of the information. We afford an intellectual cachet to anything that requires fancy tools to extract and organize. And we rely on that system to provide insight so heavily that we lose sight of what data actually *are*. Data are merely a set of quantitative or qualitative variables; where they are housed is irrelevant. Indeed, large databases with well-organized indexes and advanced query tools make it much easier to store and access information than what is gathered in our employees' experiences, but to believe that the former is capable of replacing the latter is to rob yourself—and your employees—of valuable insight.

One of the most popular examples of real-world big data is detailed in Michael Lewis's book *Moneyball*. In the book, Oakland A's general manager Billy Beane decided to forgo traditional scouting reports and took a data-driven approach to assembling the 2002 Oakland A's, much to the scout's dismay. He assembled a team without a single marquee player, and in their first year they won 103 games (including a 20-game winning streak). However, the 2002 Oakland A's did not go to the World Series. They didn't even survive the opening round of the playoffs. Did they outperform expectations? Most certainly. But there was still something missing; a data-driven roster should have been able to account for enough variables to set the team apart from everyone, right?

At the end of that season, Billy Beane received an offer to become the general manager of the Boston Red Sox, an offer he eventually declined. The Red Sox hired a different general manager; however, the owner of the Red Sox also hired an advisor named Bill James to fill a statistical gap. James was a baseball writer with a long history of analyzing baseball statistics. Many of the statistical models Billy Beane used to build the A's roster had been originally designed by Bill James; however, Bill James had distanced himself from baseball statistics years before, mostly because of the glut of statistics that he was seeing and the increasing difficulty in identifying valid trends. When he joined the Red Sox, Bill James decided to implement a slightly different approach from the one Billy Beane had used so successfully in Oakland. Instead of relying entirely on statistical data, James's new approach was a hybrid of quantitative statistical data and qualitative insight from the Red Sox scouts. Within two years, the Red Sox had won their first World Series in more than 80 years—and then they won the World Series again three years later.

Bill James understood a fundamental premise of using data to make decisions: The data you capture may not be giving you a complete picture. Indeed, James understood that the scouts whom Billy Beane had ignored were actually deep sources of data. Was that data less organized and harder to extract than the statistical data? Sure. Was it a confusing mixture of quantitative and qualitative assessments? Sure. But it was a rich data source nonetheless. It was the kind of data source that could be used to inform decisions and insights drawn from the statistical data. By bringing employees and their expertise into the decision-making process, the Boston

Red Sox were able to challenge their data-driven findings more thoroughly, search for statistical relevance in areas the data may not have initially suggested, and eventually build a team that surpassed all others—twice. The Oakland A's and Google, on the other hand, outperformed expectations while alienating and disempowering key employees.

Mistake #2: Using Data to Confirm Assumptions

At a high level, data mining is simple: It's merely a process of identifying and correlating any changes in behaviors. I can easily correlate an increase in the number of calories I eat every day with an increase in my weight. But statistics are rarely that simple. Data is generally filled with unexplained variances: spikes and dips that occur for no valid or discernible reason. It may be that we're not measuring the reason. It may be that there are too many reasons to measure. Regardless, most data sets have variances that cannot be easily explained. Data scientists call this "data noise," and they spend a lot of time explaining to their business why the sudden jump in revenue or the brief dip in sales is statistically irrelevant. Let me amend that—*good* data scientists spend time identifying "data noise"; others capitalize on it.

Nassim N. Taleb, risk engineer and author of *The Black Swan*, described the problem with variances in a big data environment this way: "I am not saying here that there is no information in big data. There is plenty of information. The problem—the central issue—is that the needle comes in an increasingly larger haystack." Taleb's point is that data sets are filled with data noise, and big data compounds that exponentially. It is enticing for managers of newly created big data environments to aggressively seek statistical correlations—to chase any variance in the data like a hound after a fox. With variances from data noise appearing regularly, it is easy to find those correlations. That ability to create false correlations is dangerous enough when data mining and searching for direction. But when we begin looking for variances in data to confirm our suspicions, it allows us to ignore lots of other relevant data, often to disastrous results.

We really only need to look back at the 2012 presidential election to find evidence of this kind of assumption-confirming misuse of big data. During that campaign, both candidates used enormous data sets to identify the voters most likely to vote for them, those most likely to vote for their opponent, and those most likely not to vote at all. Both used detailed polling numbers and statistical models to predict their margin of victory. Going into election day, both candidates had ample statistical support to show that they would, indeed, be decisively victorious.

In the end, the data gathered by President Obama's data scientists was remarkably accurate, whereas the Romney campaign's assumptions turned out to be well off the mark. It turned out the Obama campaign had sequestered their data scientists far away from campaign headquarters, where they used their data sets to create millions of double-blind theoretical models. Their technique was designed to uncover information with no preconceived notions, treating each individual voter and each voting bloc as a blank slate. The Romney campaign, on the other hand, used the same giant data sets to confirm their own assumptions about voter behavior. Independent pollsters showed that democrats would turn out in high numbers on election day. The Romney campaign assumed otherwise, and found some data to corroborate their assumption. That data turned out to be noise, and indeed, democrats showed up at the polls in much higher numbers than Romney expected. The Romney campaign assumed minorities would not show up to vote, and found some data noise to corroborate their assumption. When a record number of minorities turned out at the polls, a Romney aide said, "It just defied logic." Whether or not it defied logic, it didn't defy the big data predictions of the Obama campaign, who projected the percentage of minorities and democrats with remarkable precision.

Using big data to confirm an assumption is incomplete data science. It makes it far too easy to ignore all other relevant data in favor of our assumptions. A friend of mine once correlated the price of tomato paste and the murder rate in a major urban city for a class project. Both had grown at the same statistically higher rate than expected at exactly the same time, and yet both were data noise. Not only was the correlation between the two spikes irrelevant, but the spikes themselves were brief aberrations. It was all noise—no substance. And while that scenario seems too silly to worry about, the process is very real. The problem is that finding correlations among huge data sets filled with data noise is easy. If all you need to confirm your assumptions is to see a correlation, you will find one. But in that scenario, the data provide no actual value. A recent study of data-driven medical decisions by Dr. John Ioannidis showed that decisions made in this manner were wrong more than 8 times out of 10.

When creating our big data environment, we need to go in with the awareness that data noise exists and that every spike in the data does not have meaning. We need to understand that every correlation does not equal causation. And most importantly, when we have an assumption we want to test in the data, it should be tested multiple times under multiple variables. Valid assumptions will withstand the scrutiny, whereas completing our testing as soon as we've been proven right can be the difference between winning and losing.

Mistake #3: Sharing Too Much Data With Employees

In the customer-facing world of big data, there has been extensive debate on how to manage data that customers perceive as their own but is legally the property of the company. This idea of ownership of data bleeds into privacy rights and debates over corporate and personal ethics. With big data becoming an internal tool of companies to drive human performance, the issue of ownership is no longer in question, but the issues of perception, privacy, and ethics still remain. In an era where employers can inexpensively track every email, phone call, instant message, browser history, and mouse click, workers can be made to feel like their entire workday is under scrutiny. While there are laws to ensure certain workplace privacies, what is available to a company to aggregate and analyze is vast. While the specific knowledge of some of that data may be helpful to inform and motivate employees, others may create unintended consequences: for you, for the employee, or even for the data.

As companies begin to craft decisions based on data, the inclination is to share the entire process with employees: to show them the data points used, highlight where their individual data points measured on the spectrum of results, and showcase how the new process will affect the company. But data suffers from a version of the Hawthorne effect, which says that subjects who know they are being observed will modify their behavior as a result of the observation. Similarly, when people know they are being measured, they tend to modify the numbers. In some cases, this is a good thing. We set clear, achievable goals for employees based on leading measures of the business; these form the basis of many employees' performance reviews. They help clarify and prioritize the work process. However, as more factors begin to weigh into decision making, the ability to modify and alter behaviors becomes a danger.

In his memoir published shortly before his death in 2009, former Secretary of Defense Robert McNamara—one of the first true data wonks in government—described numerous examples of his obsessive attention to data-driven decision making. Throughout the book, he tells examples of how "loss of life" figures were the key data points to determine who was "winning" the Vietnam War. The logic behind this metric was that as loss of life grew too great on either side, morale would degrade. So McNamara incentivized the officers according to that gruesome figure. As the war continued year after year, McNamara believed that the end was always near, that the morale of the enemy was nearly broken. After all, he had the numbers to prove it. What he was unaware of was that officers, who were incentivized to report large numbers of enemy casualties, were lying. Oftentimes, the nature of war required them to guess at the number of enemy casualties, but many inflated those numbers, while others would outright lie.

The irony of the situation is that McNamara had been the CEO of Ford Motor Company before being appointed Secretary of Defense by President Kennedy. While at Ford, McNamara incentivized line managers to finish using all of the parts of one model as quickly as possible, so they could begin building the next model. The line managers complied; they dumped all the excess parts in the Delaware River.

When sharing the data we're capturing with employees, it is important to consider not only how being "observed" is going to make the employee feel, but also to consider how much a change in behavior due to that observation might affect your desired outcome. Big data allows us to make employees feel like lab rats, always under a watchful eye hidden behind a one-way mirror. Much like the Google story from earlier, the net effect of big data should never be to disempower or intimidate employees. Provided we are operating within the confines of existing privacy laws, the data we choose to share is entirely our discretion. By informing his employees of the key data points he was measuring, Robert McNamara allowed line managers at Ford and front-line officers in the war to alter their behaviors and thereby alter the data. Those changes cost Ford money in lost inventory, they cost soldiers their lives, and they greatly extended a war, all because valid decisions cannot be made from invalid data.

Mistake #4: Expecting to Uncover Predictive Analytics Quickly or Consistently

Probably the most exciting concept in big data mining is predictive analytics. With predictive analytics, companies can use existing data to identify opportunities for improvement before they happen. By avoiding known pitfalls, predictive analytics can be used to protect the bottom line, to ensure the safety of employees, or to assist in the timeliness of processes. The potential benefits of this type of analytics are large enough to justify the expense of mining big data. But that potential return-on-investment may also drive companies to demand predictive results where none are yet possible.

One of the biggest mistakes when implementing predictive analytics is an expectation of immediate or consistent results. Valid statistics don't easily mesh with the short-term, profit-driven bottom line of most business decisions. Predictive analytics work only when a clear variance is identified, correlated to another event, and validated—when we're certain an action causes a result that we do not want. As mentioned earlier, when our data sets grow larger and larger, we are guaranteed to see an increase in variances. Many of these variances may be statistically significant, although not reproducible—a one-time event that happened because of a freak set of circumstances. In a truly predictive big data environment, the set of circumstances that caused that variance would be tested over and over to ensure that specific actions always cause the undesired result. A company looking to provide an immediate return-on-investment for these efforts will usually try to force those findings. They believe that the quicker they can predict potential errors, the faster the environment pays for itself.

Unfortunately, expecting—not to mention incentivizing—those findings is a statistical misstep. Admittedly, predictive analytics is an exercise in patience: the testing and constant retesting of findings under differing variables. It is difficult to assign performance ratings to teams who go long periods without providing any usable results. However, the danger of assigning a team a goal number of usable predictors is likely to be even more costly. Companies that adopt big data with the requirement of identifying strong predictors find themselves changing course on a very regular basis, as predictors prove to be predictive only under specific circumstances.

This is not to say that predictors tested under the heaviest scrutiny may not change. Part of the responsibility of a predictive environment is to always test the predictors against the current state. As our work environments change, so do the variables that test our predictors. We have to be willing to allow for that, but to require the creation and adoption of predictors will cause us to constantly have to retool them. More often than not, a poorly-tested predictor that is put in place will be reworked until it is proven useless, which we find out only after much expense, frustration, and numerous repeats of the mistakes we were hoping to avoid.

If predictive analytics is truly being implemented to protect the bottom line, the best way to incentivize it is not by measuring the productivity of the data scientists, but by measuring the effect of the predictors on the bottom line. The advantage of predictive analytics is that it allows us to see the times when it was adopted and when it wasn't, and then gauge the impact of both groups; it is a self-contained control experiment. For instance, we know that any widget-maker who installs part B to their widget assembly before they install part A will create a faulty widget that cannot be sold. Our predictive analysis tells us that widget-makers who have an early lunch tend be tired around 4 p.m. and may accidentally grab part B before part A. Using that information, we install a system that requires all early-lunch widget-makers to acknowledge and sign off on their parts after 4 p.m. each day. Ideally, all employees will follow the new process and the number of unusable widgets will drop; our before and after numbers allow us to see the impact predictive analytics has had on the bottom line. By focusing on that impact instead of on the daily productivity of the data scientists, predictive analytics can help a company's bottom line. Patience and valid analysis are the true keys to predictive analytics success.

Avoiding These Mistakes When Implementing Big Learning Data

As big data makes its entry into training and development, these same pitfalls apply. We can use big learning data to create a continual learning environment with learning opportunities identified and embedded within individual workflows and processes. We can constantly analyze large data sets for valid statistical differences that will allow us to create learning that is more personalized, timely, and applicable. But the risks in that environment are no different than in any other data-driven environment. Poor analysis or misuse of data still runs the risk of alienating employees, confounding processes, and negatively affecting the bottom line.

One of the most common concerns of a data-driven environment is what data-driven, continual learning environments will do for needs assessment. The concern usually foresees conflicts between the actual big learning data and those in the business who know the work processes. As mentioned in mistake #1, relying on digital data only to identify training needs is closing yourself off from rich sources of data that may identify potential problems before data analysis can. More importantly for the T&D world is how these alliances can help data scientists identify what processes can and should be analyzed. Part of the solution big learning data provides is the ability to identify what tasks or processes would benefit from intervention; by bringing that personal awareness into the process, our employees and stakeholders can help identify the processes to analyze and validate. This can only occur in an environment where opinions are openly solicited and the "data" mined from our employees' collective experience is leveraged.

Once inside a culture that leverages both human experience and big data to define learning opportunities, it is important to avoid mistake #2. Poorly supported confirmation of assumptions is neither unique to big data nor to T&D, but it is a process that big data can help eliminate. Too often in the T&D world, the lack of collected data leads to decision making based on specious evidence. A single transaction goes wildly wrong and every employee must be retrained on the procedure. An irate customer threatens a lawsuit and every employee must retake compliance training. A tiny blood spill in a retail store leads to confusion about hazmat disposal, and every employee in a national chain then receives hazmat training they will never use. We allow prominent or strong incidents to bias our assumptions, and because no data has been collected around the incident, the strength of the recent incident confirms our assumption that *training is necessary*. Fortunately, a big learning data environment would be able to accurately test that assumption, and to identify the probability of the action recurring and the benefits of training for it. As the business brings training needs up, they can be velled against the big learning data—but only if the data scientists avoid the mistake of confirming assumptions.

If the goal of this process is to seamlessly embed learning into a learner's workflow, learners will also be curious what actions they are taking are being monitored, and which actions are being judged and used for performance management. As noted in mistake #3, big learning data will let us capture multiple sources of data from our learners. It is important to make sure that the data we're sharing is quantitative data that is not self-reported. Letting learners know that their actions are being observed and collected will likely increase the accuracy of the work being observed. Letting them know that data they self-report is being observed is likely to yield inflated or inaccurate data.

As we implement big learning data more often, it's important to remember that the process needs to be deliberately planned. With careful consideration and teamwork, we can ensure that we make the right decisions to provide continuous learning that is necessary, valid, and accurate.

References

Bowman, D. (2009) "Goodbye, Google." Retrieved March 20, 2009 from *stopdesign.com.*

Dickerson, J. (2012). "Why Romney Never Saw It Coming." Retrieved November 9, 2012 from *Slate.com.*

Eliot, T.S. (1934). *The Rock.* London: Faber & Faber.

Halberstram, D. (1986). *The Reckoning.* New York: William Morrow & Co.

Ioannidis, J.P.A. (2005). "Contradicted and Initially Stronger Effects in Highly Cited Clinical Research." *The Journal of the American Medical Association* 294 (2): 218–228.

Kinnard, D. (1979). *The War Managers.* Annapolis, MD: Naval Institute Press.

Lewis, M. (2003). *Moneyball.* New York: W.W. Norton & Company.

McNamara, R.S., and B. VanDeMark. (1996). *In Retrospect: The Tragedy and Lessons of Vietnam.* New York: Vintage Books.

Taleb, N.N. (2013). "Beware the Big Errors of 'Big Data'." Retrieved February 8, 2013 from *Wired* online.

CHAPTER 8

BIG LEARNING DATA RISKS

PRIVACY, TRANSPARENCY, CULTURE, AND SILLY DATA

Elliott Masie

When discussing big learning data, we must also honestly challenge the risks that it raises. Let's explore the risk side of big learning data with these phrases that might be shared by employees, managers, and even corporate lawyers:

> "I wonder how much information our employers are actively collecting on each of us? How is it being used? Can I get a copy of the big data policies of the company and even see their view of my data?"

> "As I read about the collection of data and metadata by government security and intelligence data, it raises issues about our corporate big data policies. How do we inform a new employee of the internal policies around data collection, privacy, analysis, and computer-use tracking?"

> "When is data personal, private, or shareable? If I complete a personality inventory in an HR class, such as Myers Briggs,

are my individual responses, as well as my end result, private? Once I click on a box on a corporate website, does that data become theirs or mine?"

"We have so much data now available that I don't have the time or mental bandwidth to process it all. Yet, if I don't use data analytics, does it create a legal liability for our company?"

"What happens to the culture of trust in an organization as big data becomes our operating mode?"

"I saw some charts that my manager has put together using big learning data graphics, but some of them are really silly like 'Retention Patterns for People Attending External Conferences.' He won't let us go to industry events now, because his charts show that we might get recruited. Ha! I just updated my résumé; silly managers using silly data won't keep me."

"What language should be included in our forms and courses that will add transparency and legal coverage for how we will or will not leverage the captured data and data exhaust?"

"As an instructional designer, how much big learning data can I access? It would be great to correlate learner responses on an e-learning program with demographic data such as gender, salary level, recent performance review, and even the 360-feedback from coaching! I would even love to see learning correlated with number of sick days taken in the last year. Can we see it on an anonymous and aggregated perspective?"

"When an employee is leaving our employment, what portfolio of big learning data can he take with him? In other words, how much learning and performance activity is shareable back to the worker, for feedback as well as part of his career portfolio?"

I worry about our managers using big data to create very visually interesting graphic representations of 'silly data.' Just because they can harvest the data, is it true, valuable, and helpful in decision making? We all have seen the graphs of total numbers of people trained in a year. But what does that really represent, without deeper context?"

"How will we train our employees, managers, and stakeholders on big learning data skills? What are the codes of conduct about big learning data that will create a smart, curious, and evidence-based approach to innovation and development, that is resonant with a healthy internal culture?"

"Can I opt out from some big data collections?"

"If the company is ever sued, what elements of big learning data are discoverable in court proceedings? If an employee was dismissed for poor performance, how much big learning data might she require disclosure on—for the one employee and even for a wider comparative set?"

Our goal is not to throw very cold water on the big learning data opportunity. But let's not be naïve. We must understand that big learning data is, in every sense of the word, seven things:

* **Organizational Change**—Requiring an interactive process of planning, feedback, and disclosures.

* **Privacy, Security, and Transparency Issue**—Requiring strategic, legal, and "codes of conduct" elements.

* **New Skill, Competency, and Leadership Dimension**—Requiring a learning intervention to build, assess, and develop appropriate skills.

* **Externally Referenced Phenomena**—Requiring an eye toward a greater context of how big data issues are evolving outside the workplace, including governmental, consumer, and judicial elements.

* **Experimental and Innovative Process**—Requiring iterative attempts, evidence, correction, and incubation time and reflection.

* **Values Sensitive**—Requiring alignment or sensitivity to an individual's personal, political, or even religious beliefs about privacy, openness, and individuality.

* **Globally Sensitive**—Requiring a context-specific approach that varies globally, based on culture and governmental regulations and expectations.

In the fall of 2013, it is difficult—as big learning data is just evolving—to be prescriptive about these issues. Part of the innovation process, as reflected by the authors and organizations represented in this book, is an active and open dialogue, along with collaboration on these risks. However, to add to this discussion, here are a few approaches that colleagues might consider to better align big learning data with these concerns:

* **Transparency:** Learners have the right to know how learning data will be used, shared, stored, or leveraged. We should develop a clearly stated policy so that there are no surprises about the transparency issues. It would be great if the learning industry developed a set of simple icons that would display the types of transparencies or uses that learning data will "live under" within the corporation.

* **Privacy:** Organizations may want to define areas where the privacy levels are different, or even where the learner gets to indicate the desired degree of privacy. Who gets to see the aggregated data of 1,000 learners? Who gets to see one learner's data about himself?

* **Value to the Learner:** Big learning data can provide great value back to the learner. She may want to know what other learners who have taken the same program found most difficult. What are the types of questions that she, as a learner, gets wrong the most often? What remedial actions have been most successful for other learners who failed that question or program? Which learners have had the most success with this specific instructor, based on their backgrounds or style? We must make big learning data valuable to the learner—or it will be a one-way and low-trust process.

* **Silly Data Be Gone:** There will be a major temptation by managers and even consultants to provide high-definition big data analysis

that shouts "silly data." In one sense, data is just data. So it must have context, trust, and reliability to be effective. Tracking data exhaust without context will create huge, interactive, silly data scorecards. We should develop a set of queries that helps us evaluate the meaningfulness of the evidence and conclusions. For example, people who skip all three meals in a day will lose weight, but they are not going to be healthy or live long. How do we add context and validity to our big learning data efforts?

* **Skill-Building and Collaborative Examples:** Let's define the skills, competencies, and approaches that managers, learning producers, and learners need to leverage big learning data. We should also build multi-organization collaborative efforts to provide tools, technologies, and analysis models that will push our big learning data competencies forward.

* **OK, So What Do We Do?** Big learning data will require big learning *energy.* Having a deep analysis of what helps or distracts a learner or a group of learners on the way to competency is awesome. But, that is not an answer—just a rich perspective. Now, the real issue is: OK, so what do we do now? In fact, big learning data might provide intense energy to refine, redesign, and reframe much of what an organization does in a learning effort. I bet if we analyzed the big learning data about the real impact of millions of hours of new hire orientation, we would get depressing news. Now, do we have the energy to really make those changes?

Going forward, let's approach big learning data as a new world that will have great potential and also real risks with new challenges. Ironically, let's apply big data to our approaches to big learning data. Let's evaluate the impact of big learning data from a 360-perspective and be learners about this important field.

And finally, let's value and respect the concerns, views, and opposition to big learning data from some of our colleagues. Whether they are fearful, low risk, or deeply correct in their concerns, we must be open and influenced by all perspectives on this evolving approach!

SECTION III

APPROACHES TO BIG LEARNING DATA

CHAPTER 9

CASE STUDY

IT'S BIGGER THAN BIG DATA— METRICS AND MEASUREMENT WITHOUT A STRATEGY IS JUST DATA

Nickole Hansen, Peggy Parskey, Jennifer O'Brien

Introduction

Metrics is a hot topic both in T&D and in the broader talent arena. Across all of HR, there is an increased desire to create accountability for results. In this drive for greater accountability, leading edge HR functions have concluded that decisions must be evidence-based, leveraging the gold mine of data that resides within its network of systems. HR is now squarely in the big data game, with the potential to mine its wealth of talent information to not only report but also predict outcomes based on behavioral indicators.

Unfortunately, not all talent organizations have received the message. In T&D specifically, measurement, evaluation, and analytics are often viewed as tactical activities relegated to making course by course improvement decisions. Many organizations have fallen into a dangerous trap because their business leaders are not explicitly asking for information. The reigning viewpoint is: "If no one is asking, why go through all the effort to produce reports that will likely never be reviewed or used?"

Their skepticism is fair. How many reports are generated each year and what is actually done with them? Do the recipients want them? Are the data useful? Are they presented in a format that is meaningful to the recipient? Do they answer important questions, for example: Are we using resources efficiently? Are we producing high-quality solutions that improve the performance of our employees? Are we making a positive impact on business results?

For most T&D organizations, their big data are just data. At Grant Thornton, in the last 12 months alone, we gathered more than 750,000 evaluation question responses. Add that to our LMS, HR, and T&D financial data, and it is clear that we are not suffering from a lack of data. Our challenge, however, was to transform this big data into big insights and to do that, we needed both a strategy and a tactical plan. This case study shares the Grant Thornton journey as we transformed our measurement and along the way, recognized that it is "bigger than big data."

Background

Under the direction of CLO Mark Stutman, our learning leaders collaboratively developed a learning strategy to guide our team over the next few years. Gathering the national learning leaders and select national heads of practice, we defined our mission, vision, and drivers. The team grappled with tough questions like, "Why aren't we producing better business professionals?" and "Why aren't we visibly demonstrating an impact on the business?" As we answered these questions, we realized that we needed to change our training and development approach.

In our strategy-development process, we committed to building the necessary competencies and capabilities to enhance performance and our competitive advantage. Additionally, we agreed that metrics and analytics must support this new strategy to ensure the learning organization provides value to the firm. One pillar of the overall learning strategy focused on measurement and stated that we would "invest in learning with demonstrative value." While simple to say, we realized that this one statement, in and of itself, implied a high degree of change. We needed to determine how to:

* Measure not just the efficiency, effectiveness, and impact of our programs, but also of the entire learning function.

* Transform measurement from an after-the fact tactical activity to a strategic process that informs annual investment planning.

* Engage the business throughout our solution design and development process, and create a culture of mutual accountability for results.

* Enable T&D to operate like a business.

These considerations led us to realize that we had to go beyond the concept of big data. We needed a separate but aligned measurement strategy. Moreover, this strategy needed to be supported and driven collaboratively by T&D as well as the firm's leaders.

Before developing the measurement strategy, we embarked on a communication campaign. We met with our learning steering committee, senior leadership, and the CEO to socialize the key learning initiatives. This process built the needed top-level support.

Our goal was to ensure the firm leaders understood the importance of a measurement strategy and to engage them in the process for change. This level of commitment helped us to gain valuable input and accelerate our process. Once we had their buy-in, we were ready to initiate the measurement-strategy development process.

We can't solve problems by using the same kind of thinking we used when we created them.

—Albert Einstein

Bring the Best Resources

Getting senior leadership buy-in was an important first step that also carried with it a great responsibility to get it right. We had driven numerous projects in the past but had no one on staff who was a true expert in learning measurement. After spending months researching, reading books, and speaking with industry leaders, we remembered a quote by Albert Einstein: "We can't solve problems by using the same kind of thinking we used when we created them."

A transformation of our strategic learning function required new and fresh thinking. We needed to bring in experts in measurement to guide us and bring credibility to the work. Because our leaders believed strongly in what we were doing and we had already laid the groundwork, we were able to engage KnowledgeAdvisors, a talent analytics firm, to help us develop our measurement strategy.

Figure 4: EVALUATION MODEL WITH EIGHT KEY DIMENSIONS

Developing a Measurement Strategy

KnowledgeAdvisors takes a unique approach to its measurement strategy effort. They realize that changing how, when, what, and why organizations measure their results requires more than technology and amassing data. Based on work by Jay Galbraith, they have designed an evaluation model comprised of eight key dimensions (see Figure 4). When all dimensions are implemented, Grant Thornton will have created sustainable measurement and evaluation within the organization. Equally importantly, the evaluation practices will drive greater efficiency and effectiveness within the learning function and will produce greater value for the organization.

When KnowledgeAdvisors presents this model, they reference a table adapted from Galbraith that demonstrates the importance of each dimension to the overall health of an organization's evaluation system (see Table 1).

Table 1: MAPPING THE IMPORTANCE OF EACH DIMENSION TO ORGANIZATIONAL SYSTEMS

Dimension	If:	Then:	Impact
Leadership/ Governance	no senior leadership oversight for measurement	**confusion**	• no criteria for decision making • difficult to get enterprise-wide adherence
Processes	lacking an integrated end to end process for measurement	**misaligned goals**	• misallocation of resources to programs • delayed insights into value of programs on business outcomes.
Roles/ Accountabilities	measurement accountability not clarified for process stakeholders or learning practitioners	**loss of focus**	• lack of process oversight • no mutual commitment to drive outcomes
Skills & Behaviors	people not trained or competent in measurement	**low performance**	• misuse of measurement and evaluation methods • misinterpretation of data
Standards/Tools	people are not enabled	**wasted effort**	• nonvalue added variation in measurement • inability to aggregate or slice/ dice data
Technology	multiple or no common platforms	**fragmentation**	• inability to integrate data • loss of capacity due to manual manipulation of data
Results Utilization	data doesn't drive decisions	**gridlock**	• long decision and cycle time • difficult to continually improve
Culture	doesn't reinforce desired behavior	**inertia**	• reversion to old behaviors • decisions driven by gut versus evidence

Adapted from "Designing Dynamic Organizations," Galbraith, Downey, Kates, 2002.

KnowledgeAdvisors makes the case that too many organizations focus on two or three dimensions: typically the technology to gather large amounts of data efficiently and cost effectively; standards to enable comparisons to benchmarks; and reporting to deliver results quickly to stakeholders. They explained that this approach is superb at providing a large supply of data to the organization but does not address the demand side of the equation. Organizations fall into the trap of big data but gain small to no insights, because they lack: leaders who require quality and meaningful data for decisions; an integrated process that requires success measures at the outset, and a culture that is data driven.

Developing the Strategy

To establish the strategy, KnowledgeAdvisors used a three-phase process. The process began with a current state assessment to determine Grant Thornton's capabilities in learning measurement. The second phase focused on the future state to identify our aspirations for measurement and the capabilities we expect to establish within a three-year horizon. The final phase built the strategy and road map to close the gap between the current and desired states. The road map provides detailed tactical implementation steps to guide our measurement activities and investments to realize the future state.

Current State of Measurement at Grant Thornton

Our current state assessment involved consultants interviewing T&D leaders as well as our senior business leadership team and the CEO. The involvement of business leaders was critical and ensured that our measurement strategy would incorporate the voice of the business in our long-term approach. The consultants also deployed their proprietary maturity diagnostic tool to gather quantitative data in addition to the qualitative interview data.

The results did not surprise our learning leadership, and in fact validated what most had observed in their day-to-day work.

KnowledgeAdvisors identified key strengths in our organization, including:

* a strong desire for measuring the impact of learning, not only by T&D leaders, but equally important, by business leaders

* wide use of scorecards and reports to drive program level improvements

* a single, common technology platform to collect learning evaluation data

* a standardized learning management and compliance-tracking system.

At the same time, KnowledgeAdvisors recommended areas for improvement:

* Integrate measurement into the existing learning design and development process.

* Enhance measurement and evaluation capability of the team.

* Develop a set of balanced, common, consistent measures across the organization that demonstrate our efficiency, effectiveness, and impact on the business.

* Optimize our technology platform to simplify use, enable robust reporting, and employ scalable methods to demonstrate business impact.

Throughout the process, our consultants captured comments and feedback. A theme emerged from this qualitative feedback: Just having the data doesn't get you where you need to be.

* "We don't do a lot with the data. We have systems in place, but don't do a lot with the information we are collecting."

* "I have data, but not a whole lot of information."

We clearly needed to rethink what we provide, how we use information, and how we tell the story to communicate the value of learning.

A Compelling Future State and a Plan to Get There

The next phase of the process was to develop a future-state vision of measurement within our T&D organization. Our consultants facilitated a half-day visioning session with the senior T&D leadership team. Divided into subgroups, the team was given a challenge: Articulate world-class measurement along each key dimension of the maturity model. What would be different in this new world? How would our role in T&D change, and what would we be doing differently?

Our brainstorming envisioned a strong partnership with the business anchored in a value of mutual accountability. We will leverage the discipline of performance consulting to ensure that training is the appropriate solution, but equally important, we will establish success measures and outcome goals for all solutions before we begin design or development. In our future state, our organization will have a metrics mentality, making decisions based on credible, accessible, and meaningful data and information. Our governance will be both bottom-up and top-down, incorporating the voice of the business and the voice of our learners. Finally, the data we gather, synthesize, analyze, and report will enable us to manage T&D, demonstrate our impact on the business, and provide meaningful insights to both T&D and business leaders.

The final phase of the strategy-development process was to develop the tactical plan. This effort focused on three phases of work:

* demonstrating short-term quick wins to ensure that we optimized our existing investment in technology

* leveraging our new performance consulting rollout to change the conversation with the business

* aligning our T&D measures with the critical few measures identified by our CEO and senior leaders.

Our short-term effort also focused on establishing a single owner for executing the tactical plan. As we establish our mid- and long-term plans, we will focus on building measurement maturity and creating a data-driven culture. Our success with our strategy will be measured by increased organizational capability in measurement; pervasive use of our data to inform operational, program, and strategic decisions; and a strong partnership with the business.

Final Thoughts

For those who are struggling with big data overload, it is important to remember that data does not drive business. How data is used will make the difference in how impactful your organization will be to drive results. To harness the power of the data, you need to think bigger and start with a strategy.

Key insights from our strategy development:

* Get leadership involved early. Involving business leaders in the process will help to gain support for your work and ensure that you are aligning with the business strategy.

* Look holistically at all the dimensions that affect measurement. The data and measures are important—however, if you don't look at other areas which affect the demand of the data, such as leadership and utilization, then you will be missing a key ingredient for success.

* Begin small and build. If you wait to have everything in place, you may never start. Take small steps, look for quick wins, and plan for continual improvement.

Grant Thornton is on a journey as we execute on our measurement strategy to advance our measurement maturity. We have our sights set to utilize the abundance of data in a more meaningful way. The strategy is the foundation to ensure that we are using our data to make informed strategic decisions, to increase learning with a demonstrative value.

CHAPTER 10

BIG DATA, BIG DIFFERENCE IN TRAINING AND DEVELOPMENT

Jeff Losey

Imagine the Possibilities

Imagine the possibilities of a system that enables your organization to merge data from multiple sources: 360-degree survey feedback, performance ratings, key performance indicators, quality and customer service scores, efficiency ratings, engagement feedback, external sites and databases, and more. The system then makes these data available to help your employees design individualized professional development plans by targeting their personal and professional development opportunities, identifying and enlisting mentors, tracking progress, and making themselves visible to hiring managers when that perfect career opportunity opens up anywhere inside the company. Doesn't this sound like a tool that would deliver significant organizational impact?

It's exactly what we're building today in the Professional Development Center at the University of Farmers, Claims.

Bringing Big Data and Development Together

Our new Professional Development Center (PDC) application brings multiple internal and external data sources together in one proprietary online tool, and uses that data to help our employees assess how they measure up against the 57 skills, 14 competencies, and five major themes we've identified as mission-critical to the Farmers organization.

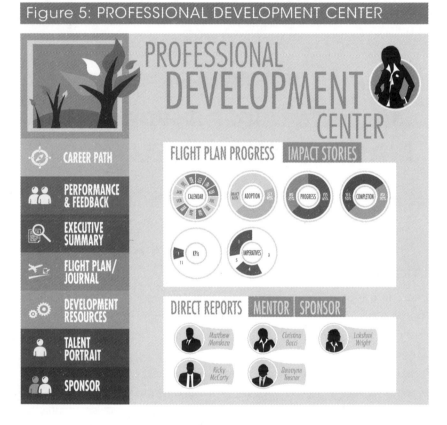

Figure 5: PROFESSIONAL DEVELOPMENT CENTER

PDC enables every employee to design, track, discuss, and share their performance and personal growth with others in the organization. It drives individual improvement by helping employees find and access training and development resources both inside the company and across the Internet, and by helping employees build their own development and career networks. It also creates company-wide visibility for every employee so that the most qualified, prepared individuals get noticed—and considered—when an appropriate job opens up anywhere in the organization.

For the organization, bringing multiple data sources together in the PDC tool means that we can deliver personalized learning more efficiently and effectively, by getting the right content and information into each learner's hands at the moment and location of need, and deliver a positive impact on organizational goals and priorities in the process.

Figure 6: CLAIMS KPIS & IMPERATIVES

— Claims KPI

— Targeted employee training

— Professional Development Center

— Claims Imperatives

In short, PDC is a one-stop shop for every Farmers Claims employee's individual training and development needs—and a key driver of the Claims organization's overall performance and business results.

What PDC Does

PDC supports our employees' skills and competencies improvement over time by aggregating each person's data in an individualized executive summary. Participants discuss the executive summary with their immediate supervisor and their peers before developing their own developmental "flight plan." PDC also enables them to identify and connect with mentors whose identified area of strength is their key area for development—so a voluntary, highly personalized, and carefully targeted mentoring component.

Figure 7: MENTORSHIP

Search for a mentor strong in: ROLE MODELING OUR NORMS AND VALUES

SEARCH RESULTS

Christina Bacci ★★★ Matthew Mondoza ★★★★ Dewayne Tresner ★★ Lakshmi Wright ★★★

Once the flight plan is drafted, it's posted on each employee's individual dashboard in PDC, where they, their supervisor, and their mentors can access it.

PDC then tracks and records progress toward completion of specific skill and interpersonal development objectives set forth in the flight plan; measures the impact of that progress on targeted skills and competencies; and links those achievements to the organization's strategic imperatives and key performance indicators (for example, quality, customer service, and efficiency). In effect, the system correlates individual development with company-wide performance results to deliver a real-time snapshot of how individual employee growth is helping drive organizational improvement.

Figure 8: DEVELOPMENTAL FLIGHT PLAN

By adopting a flight plan, making progress toward completion, and including KPIs and organizational imperatives in your development actions, each participant drives organizational impact.

It also gives employees a built-in journaling tool, which they, their supervisor, and their mentors can use to document follow-up on developmental goals, note personal successes, recognize "slips" in their personal progress, and post statements about their efforts, intentions, and achievements. All of this holds them accountable for their personal progress, making their thought processes transparent to their supervisor and mentors, and boosting engagement in their growth journey.

PDC also provides links to numerous training and development resources, both inside Farmers and on the Internet, including books, videos, stretch assignments, and exercises. And its learning communities tool enables employees to engage in connected learning by sharing insights with and learning from other Farmers colleagues working on the same personal strengths and opportunities.

We have three key rules for the content of each employee's flight plan. The action or development opportunity must be:

* Good for the individual—linked to the greatest opportunity identified in their executive summary.

* Good for the company—in concert with Farmers' strategic themes, with development actions tied to the company's KPIs.

* A priority for Claims—in clear alignment with our strategic imperatives.

Interestingly, the PDC application itself demonstrates perfect alignment with those imperatives, which call for Farmers Claims to:

* Be an organization of results-based exemplary leaders.

* Invest in the quality of our workforce.

* Employ industry-leading technology.

* Foster a culture of continuous improvement.

* Develop robust analytical capabilities and data-driven insights into the business.

Because PDC is not used as a performance assessment or performance-rating tool, it offers a safe environment in which Claims employees can collaborate, learn, and grow.

PDC also represents an important cultural shift for Farmers. We don't want to tell individual employees what we think their career path ought to be, and direct them to what we think would be the right training and development opportunities for them—other than essential training in claims handling and customer service responsibilities, of course. We want our employees to have the power to consider, design, and pursue the career path they're each most interested in. We provide the tool. Then it is up to each employee to decide how to use that tool as they plan and pursue their professional goals.

Figure 9: FEEDBACK

FEEDBACK

Feedback data determines
your real professional self.

DEVELOPMENT GAP

Development bridges the gap between
the professional you are now and the
one you want to become.

Big Data and Career Opportunities

Just how does PDC help Farmers Claims employees identify and pursue the career opportunities it has helped them prepare for?

In addition to making each employee's executive summary and flight plan visible—allowing hiring managers to get to know a person on paper, learn something about their skills and opportunities and their personal and professional goals, and assess where they've progressed on their growth journey—the PDC application also allows each employee to post and maintain a talent portrait on their dashboard. This gives hiring managers a common, comprehensive view of all candidates, delivered in the same format and with the same package of information, leveling the playing field among employees, many of whom the hiring manager may never have met or worked with before.

And the information that a hiring manager is using has, by virtue of the PDC content development process, been heavily vetted and validated by input from multiple sources. So it's a far more accurate and unbiased source of information about a job candidate's skills and opportunities, competencies and interests, and current personal development focus, than any of the single stand-alone sources of information traditionally used in corporate America to consider candidates and assess their fit for a job opening.

Hiring managers can also dig into the data housed in PDC to search for candidates, refining their search by sorting for current line of business, experience in other internal business disciplines, salary grade, performance rating, language skills, mobility, interest in technical versus leadership career paths, supervisor and peer evaluations, executive sponsors and mentors, and more. This enables them to create much broader, Claims-wide succession pools of fully vetted candidates who meet specific job criteria and are ready for their next role.

PDC and Organizational Learning Initiatives

When it comes to using PDC to deliver learning opportunities to employees, the system enables Farmers to deploy our resources far more efficiently than before. Here's how.

Using system data, we analyze the skills that our people are working on individually, to identify which of the 57 skills underlie our employees' most frequently pursued opportunity areas.

That enables our Learning Design and Curation team to focus its efforts on the areas of greatest need in the organization as they build new learning initiatives. It also gives our Learning Delivery team crucial information about the specific skills, competencies, and behavioral opportunities they should focus on in delivering classroom, webinar, online, social, and mobile-learning sessions.

Additionally, system data helps us identify geographic "clusters" of employees who are working on the same development opportunity. That enables us to send a member of the Learning Delivery team out to deliver highly customized, targeted, group instruction and coaching when face-to-face learning is the preferred option. And, of course, we encourage each group of learners to establish communities in PDC so they continue to partner with each other as they build skill and competency in their shared focus area.

But we don't neglect our employees whose personal training and development objectives lie outside of the major areas of interest identified in PDC. System data help us link those individuals with a comprehensive set of online learning resources, either created internally or culled by our Learning Design and Curation staff from the panoply of options available online, and delivered via Internet to our employees.

Whether it's live, connected, or e-learning that's needed, PDC helps us identify that need and efficiently deliver the most effective learning solution.

Finally, PDC offers access to training at the moment of need, allowing each employee to search for, locate, and use precisely the information they need, when it's absolutely critical to their performance, wherever they happen to be working that day.

Looking Ahead

As we complete the rollout of PDC to all Claims executive, managerial, supervisory, and pre-supervisory line employees this year, we're already thinking about next steps, including building our nine-box analysis of each employee's readiness for their next career opportunity, and information about an employee's career sponsors and current job successors, into the system.

We're also preparing to aggregate system data on mentors and sponsors, to help us assess their skill at identifying and developing talent, to better hold managers accountable for their hiring and promotional decisions, and to help us identify people we want to develop as master mentors and sponsors. All of this will further strengthen our ability to foster our employees' career development.

And we're preparing to loop back to employees who participated in the first waves of the PDC rollout last year. All Claims employees are automatically invited to complete a new 360-degree survey every 18 months to ensure that they periodically rethink their executive summary and flight plan. Employees who move into a new job spend six months in that new role and then participate in a new 360 degree survey, executive summary, and flight-plan creation process.

Figure 10: SPONSORSHIP

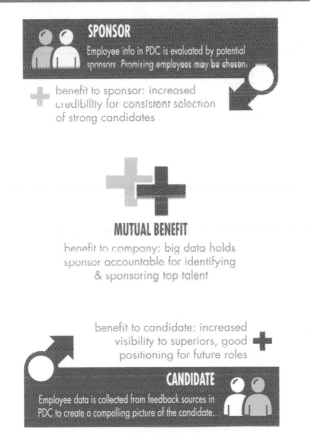

SPONSOR
Employee info in PDC is evaluated by potential sponsors. Promising employees may be chosen.

benefit to sponsor: increased credibility for consistent selection of strong candidates

MUTUAL BENEFIT
benefit to company: big data holds sponsor accountable for identifying & sponsoring top talent

benefit to candidate: increased visibility to superiors, good positioning for future roles

CANDIDATE
Employee data is collected from feedback sources in PDC to create a compelling picture of the candidate.

We don't expect any employee to make earth-shatteringly huge leaps in skill, competence, or personal development as a result of the work they do in PDC. What we are looking for is incremental progress for all employees that positively affects the company. We want everyone to think about it as if they're taking a bite out of the apple every month or two—making gradual and noticeable progress toward their personal and professional goals, and improving their behavior in a way that boosts their own and their team's performance and builds their organizational network.

By delivering usable data from multiple sources to help every employee in the Farmers Claims organization develop themselves and structure a program that moves them down the career path they most want to pursue, the Professional Development Center will boost efficiency, lower our expense ratio, improve the quality of our people's work, and deliver claims service that truly wows our customers. And that will enable the University of Farmers, Claims to demonstrate with cold, hard data how significant and positive an impact learning and professional development can indeed have on a corporation.

"It's been a wonderful experience!"

A manager in Farmers' Property line of business, Daniel Mesaros is a strong advocate of the company's new Professional Development Center application. When he goes into the PDC tool to post a journal note, update his developmental flight plan, or converse with other employees in a community, he says,"I never feel like it's something I have to do. It's not part of my review…I'm not being critiqued on my performance. I'm partnering with people on my development."

Mesaros, who worked for more than eight years at Farmers, then for two other insurers before returning almost 10 years ago, thinks PDC is unlike any other performance-planning tool he's used. "Other tools I've used were never functional for me. With PDC, I wrote a thorough purpose statement for myself, and I keep updating it regularly.

"I use the competencies I identified in discussions with my manager every month," he added. "Am I spending my time wisely? Am I doing things to support the leadership model? Am I focusing on innovation?"

Those conversations are easier, Mesaros adds, than developmental discussions of old, "because they're a partnership between people. You want your partners to have information that's useful. Now, my manager and I swap books on topics like leadership and innovation."

"In the past, when someone would, for example, critique a presentation I'd given, it wouldn't always sit well. Now, it's a conversation instead of a review. My manager will say, 'I was reading a book on that…you might benefit from it.' And if I put it in my flight plan as an action, I'm account-able for getting it read."

Building a Personal Brand Image

As John Bilek, leader of Missouri and Kansas Auto at Farmers, explains it, the Professional Development Center application helps each employee "control how others will perceive you. It enables you to build and promote your own brand image. How you present yourself—how you've written and updated your developmental flight plan, the photo you've chosen…did you just put any photo up there or is it professional and carefully cropped—it all sets the tone for the type of person you are and the perceptions people have of you."

It also keeps you focused on your own development, he says. "In PDC, you're sharing your development plan with the person you report to, your mentors, and anyone who may be interested in you. When a plan just sits in a folder on your desktop, it's not visible. Our old tools and methods didn't make development seem important."

PDC also "helps you keep on target. I use journaling, periodic supervisor reviews, and the pie chart visuals to monitor my progress toward development goals. These all help me confirm that I'm moving forward in my own personal development."

The 360-degree survey component was "a humbling experience," Bilek added. "It opened my eyes…is that really how I'm being perceived?! I identified 'clarity of message' and 'listening' as two key developmental areas from the feedback I received."

And it's working. "When I started using PDC, 40 percent of the people who offered feedback said that I listened well. I just asked the same question again after a year, and 90 percent of the people said I've significantly improved my listening skills."

CHAPTER 11

CASE STUDY

POINTS FOR THE TRAINING SCOREBOARD

Ben Morrison

Introduction

This chapter is all about one training department's plan to use existing big data to achieve a better evaluation of training department efficiency and effectiveness. Before we get into what data we have and how to organize it, it's probably a good idea to review what we do for our organization as a whole.

Training is all about giving people the tools to perform. It starts with a need identified by an organization to prepare new employees to contribute, through work, for the first time. It is also done to refresh existing employee skills so they can perform in a new or a better way. By the end of a training event, the learner should not only feel more confident, but they should also be able to apply what they've learned to the job and thereby improve organizational performance.

Arguably, we've gotten pretty good at measuring how confident learners are; however, most of us struggle getting proof that trainees actually have the skills and knowledge necessary to be successful on the job. Sometimes we measure those attributes during or right after a training event through skill and knowledge checks. But it takes a lot more effort to measure skills as they are applied to a job when you approach that measurement in the traditional manner.

The reasons that we struggle in measuring skill transfer to the workplace are various. Many of the issues have to do with access. Training is often planned, developed, and delivered in places far away from where the work occurs. Even if the work took place right outside our windows, we still wouldn't have the human resources or time to take the sample measures necessary to have full confidence that training had stuck.

In our department, we train airline employees that work in airports, call centers, support centers, and offices all over the United States, and recently we've added a few neighboring countries to the mix. To complicate matters further, we have little control over what happens in the interim between the training and when work begins.

The other measures that could benefit our department are related to our own internal efficiencies. Here are just a few metrics we would like to get better at measuring:

* reaction
* learning
* job transfer
* impact
* estimated ROI.

Our training department is responsible for training more than 40,000 employees. That is a huge undertaking for a staff of around 200. The good news is that we have countless data points that are almost at our fingertips. I say "almost" because the ones that are important to us are not readily apparent. Before we do anything else with data mining, we have to find out which data points are relevant by solving some pretty tough mysteries.

Figure 11: ENHANCED TRAINING DASHBOARD

Enhanced Training Dashboard

Instr Utiliz	Developer Utiliz	Classroom Utiliz	Budget Perf
75%	83%	89%	98%

Dev/Delivery Ratio	Delivery Consistency	SH Satisfaction	Ontime
55:1	98% ⬆	97% ⬆	95% ⬆

Learning Solutions				Projects In Development	YTD Learning Hours
D	OL	ILT	blend	28	550,000

Reaction Metric	Learning Metric	Job Transfer	Impact Metric	Estimated ROI
4.8	4.1	3.5	4.0	125%

Proposed dashboard—the numbers shown here are not actual.

One mystery comes from the fact that data points are all around us, and they are constantly changing and interacting in new ways to create even more information to interpret. The good news is that the means of collecting, crunching, and organizing data are getting easier through technology, but the bad news is that figuring out what is important to collect has actually become somewhat clouded because there is so much more data to choose from.

To clear the air, we have to ask the right questions first. The right questions are invariably related to what is important to our business. In the case of an airline, the big ticket items that training has an impact on are things like safety, customer service, efficiency (which leads to lower cost, which drives a lot of other metrics our shareholders care about), and employee satisfaction. If we don't understand how well our training is transferring to the job, the other metrics have much less value.

There is very little opportunity to see how well learning survives between a training event and job performance. Yet, there are hundreds, if not thousands, of potential influencers of the metrics we care about as a training department. This is the challenge set before us.

The Trainer's Challenge

Most training professionals are familiar with Donald Kirkpatrick's four levels of evaluation (plus, there is a fifth which relates to ROI). Here is a simple mnemonic device I learned years ago from a fellow co-worker:

LLUD it

Level 1 – Did they **like** it?

Level 2 – Did they **learn** it?

Level 3 – Do they **use** it (on the job)?

Level 4 – Does it make a **difference**?

Almost all training professionals are pretty familiar with designing measures for levels 1 and 2. I've encountered very few examples where level 3 is even attempted, and even fewer that are successful. Level 4, using quantitative data, is rarer still.

Big data has been defined earlier in this book; however, we should also consider how it might relate to training evaluation. Since big data contains many sources of independent data that can interact in unique and unpredictable ways, standard database tools and techniques are inadequate to handle them. Also, time adds complexity that can add another level to the analysis.

An organization of Southwest Airlines' size surely has big data. We know that big data is a growing trend in many industries and government. You may have heard that Facebook can accurately predict your political affiliation, among other things, simply by using your browsing, comments, and "like" history on its site. Many people fear the collection of personal data and the conclusions that may be drawn from it. They fear it for privacy reasons, but also because they can't control who has access, and they sometimes cannot easily erase the data.

Also, in the news is the story of the NSA contractor and whistleblower turned espionage fugitive, Edward Snowden, who claims that the NSA was collecting huge amounts of wireless phone data along with gaining access to social media and browser data. The NSA admitted data were collected, but said only data from people suspected of having terrorist connections were analyzed further. There is certainly more to come on this story. Whatever you think or feel about the situation, it should add a level of caution to our use of big data and how we handle it when it is collected.

For the purpose of evaluating training, we can take special steps to mask or preclude certain data bits that have nothing to do with helping us understand how well training survived its journey to the worksite. Training is not typically an accountability part of the organization, so knowing *who* failed to perform is not as important as *why* they failed.

Finding the Data

Enough of the heavy stuff—let's get back to training evaluation. Suppose that we have level 1 and 2 evaluations in place and would be happy with adding a level 3 evaluation for a training program. How would we go about getting that? To start, we need a means to find out what employees are doing on the job after training. A traditional approach would be to require a random sample of observations of people doing the job in question. That would require training and calibration of the observers so they would know what to look for. The results would be in the form of a somewhat objective and quantitative set of data. If the sample size was large enough and we controlled for extraneous variables, we could reasonably attribute the job performance to training. There could also be some qualitative data that is captured during the observations. In other words, the observers would be able to provide information that tells how well the employees were applying the skills learned. They could also pick up on how much the employees liked or disliked the skills they were being asked to apply. They would be able to see if other tasks interfered with the task being observed, and so on.

You might ask, "Why can't we just survey the employees and ask if they are applying their new skills to the job?" Well, some people tell you the truth and some don't, and it is nearly impossible to tell the difference. The reasons some people are dishonest are pretty obvious. One reason is employees recognize the effort and cost that went into training and don't want to admit they are taking shortcuts. Supervisors are biased observers; if they admitted their employees are doing their jobs incorrectly, it would seem to reflect badly on their leadership. If you pick up any book on survey methods, you'll get a brain full of how bias can invalidate the results of a well-constructed survey.

So, surveying isn't objective enough and sample observations are costly and inefficient. Our third option is to look at data that indicate proper or poor job performance. We're still working on just how we will go about doing that. However, we do know that many departments collect data from the workplace. Here are just a few pieces of information that are potential targets for us to use:

* training histories
* LMS data
* training assessments (level 2)
* in-class quiz and skill checks
* on-time performance
* aircraft turn times
* overtime
* absenteeism
* aircraft damage
* irregularity reporting
* hours paid per trip
* counter-line wait times
* aircraft check data
* repair histories
* error reporting
* maintenance inspection data
* technology support-call data
* safety audits
* injury reports
* compliance audits
* customer experience surveys
* internal commendations
* customer compliments
* customer complaints
* customer letters
* center quality ratings
* average call handle time
* average wait time
* abandon rate
* supervisor performance reports
* hire data
* performance reviews
* exit data
* performance improvement plans
* FMLA
* other HR data (work experience)
* log of support calls where improper procedure was used
* bag wait times
* lost and damaged baggage reports.

There are many more data sources we have yet to identify. The key for us is to find measures that are taken in an objective, comprehensive, and consistent manner.

Organizing the Data

The hard work begins. First, we will try to learn how each data type is collected, organized, and saved. How we access and use our newfound data is going to depend on the questions we ask and which data points are most likely to have a relationship with that data. I am currently exploring a couple of methods to test for putting points on our scoreboard. The first is called causal modeling and uses regression analysis to explain the relationship between several variables and the outcome. The other is the experimental method where we control a variable, as much as possible, during rollout to statistically determine if that variable had an impact.

Causal models usually begin with diagrams of inferred relationships between variables. The models can be tested to determine a relationship between multiple variables and an outcome. In our case, we're looking for the relationship between training data and good (or bad) performance. We can also easily throw in other variables that we think have a causal relationship with the outcome variable.

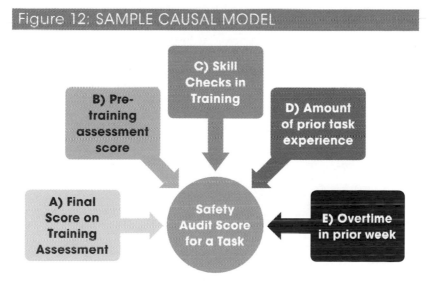

Figure 12: SAMPLE CAUSAL MODEL

The outcome variable in this example would be a safety audit. We would look to understand the causal relationship between training and the performance of a task on the job, as measured from a safety perspective. Variables A, B, and C all would come from our training records. Variables D, E, and other nontraining variables that might have a relationship with the outcome would have to come from HR or payroll records. If it turns out that training has a weak relationship with the safety task while experience has a strong relationship, we now have information we can use to beef up our training. If it turns out that training has a strong relationship with task performance, but the amount of overtime in the prior week also has a strong influence on how well they did the task, that is information we can pass on to the operational leadership.

We can use experimental methods to compare groups that receive different treatment during training. This doesn't necessarily need a lot of data sources, but it can isolate specific variables that may relate to outcome.

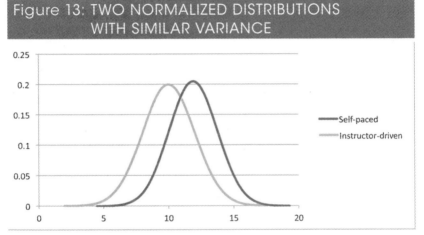

Figure 13: TWO NORMALIZED DISTRIBUTIONS WITH SIMILAR VARIANCE

Figure 13 shows two normalized distributions with similar variance, where statistics could show whether there was a meaningful difference between two groups. We could use this method to see if there is a difference in impact on task performance between two classroom approaches, like instructor-driven classroom learning versus self-paced learning with a classroom coach. The performance data would possibly come from one of the big data measurements listed earlier (for example, center quality rating). A note of caution: This method can be subject to sampling errors. For example, if by chance we happened to get a sample of very high performers in one of the groups, we could end up with an erroneous result (so, a statistically significant difference between groups that was not related to the variable at all). Random assignment to groups helps to minimize this error, but that also adds complexity to the process.

The quantitative approaches above mostly address one area of our dashboard, which is level 3 evaluation. This is our most complex challenge and is most likely to benefit from a big data strategy. SH (Stakeholder) satisfaction might be another complex stat to get, since stakeholder satisfaction can be influenced by so many factors. Knowing what factors influence stakeholder satisfaction could help us maximize our entire department's performance from a customer service perspective. The other areas of our enhanced dashboard like "instructor utilization," shown on Figure 11, can be managed with more traditional data-monitoring tools. Complex statistical methods are probably unnecessary for these other areas.

Once we get our feel wet with our primary questions about training transfer and job impact, we can start to explore other questions that big data might be able to answer. One question that comes to mind is correlating success in training with hiring data. That information could really help us enhance our hiring practices, highlighting certain indicators that lead to more successful employees. In addition, we could look for factors that predict failure and tweak the training to help more of those people succeed.

We also could turn the data digging a little more inward and discover what factors lead to better development, instruction, and delivery methods. We can also turn our scopes outward and look at the universe of data outside of our organization to see what might be affecting our success.

Conclusions

It is our responsibility to care about and understand the solutions we create. This underscores a strong need to measure the impact training has on our company's operation. We can no longer afford to be satisfied with smile sheets and multiple-choice exam results. In order to take it to the next level (level 3), we have to get a handle on better analysis tools and find ways to access data which were previously used in one-dimensional ways.

Our first customers are the employees who attend our training. They have a right to receive training that helps keep them safe and productive. If we are providing the right skills and knowledge for our first customer, our second customer (the organization) will also be satisfied. We have a tough job and we need to learn new ways to measure and analyze data so we can continually improve our training methods. First, we have to find which bits of data are likely to be relevant for analysis. Then, we have to make sure that training impact is measured consistently and comprehensively so we can trust the results. Finally, we have to safeguard the data so we aren't singling out individuals for undue attention or punitive measures.

References

Fisher, R.A. (1971). *The Design of Experiments,* 8th edition. New York: Hafner Publishing Company.

Kirkpatrick, D. (1998). *Evaluating Training Programs.* San Francisco: Berrett-Koehler Publishers.

Mike2.0. (2013). "Big Data Definition." Retrieved on September 9, 2013 from http://mike2.openmethodology.org/wiki/Big_Data_Definition.

CHAPTER 12

CASE STUDY

BIG LEARNING DATA
SOURCES AND ANALYTICS

Doug Armstrong

Introduction

Obviously, technology has afforded the learning field many advantages. As previously mentioned in this book, big data can be leveraged to understand the true value of an organization's learning assets. As the learning field moves closer to a learning-for-one model, big data analysis will become increasingly important to understanding the needs of an increasingly granular goal. In turn, we have the opportunity to analyze big data sets in aggregate to develop a clearer understanding of the value of the design, relevancy, and business impact of learning.

I became involved in big data analysis through my work in leveraging web analytics to better understand how to optimize electronic performance support systems (EPSS). I soon began to realize the value of web analytics to improving EPSS, and from there extrapolated what this could mean to enhancing all learning modalities through the aggregate of different data streams. From this assumption, I expanded my thinking toward what these data sets could tell us about learners and their individual needs. With this in mind, I am currently working on a proof-of-concept to develop a measurement strategy that incorporates web analytic data, LMS data, multimedia data, demographic data, performance data, and on-the-job performance data to assess the effectiveness of a big learning data strategy. The point to keep in mind is the potential and possibilities of analyzing various data sets to create a more complete picture of not only our learning and support offerings, but of our learners as well.

Our Approach

As we move forward with our proof-of-concept, the following represents ways that data can be used to understand learning assets in terms of their impact on people, and in turn what the impact of people's usage of these resources can tell us about the value of them. I assume a full implementation of all learning strategies, including: classroom, web-based training, LMS, performance support, multimedia, and self-directed/informal learning, as well as business operational resources like performance management tools, employee management tools, and customer relation support tools. For this proof-of-concept I put aside the organization's ability to capture and aggregate these data streams, as well as the legal and privacy implications of this strategy, and simply focus on defining a comprehensive strategy and some thoughts on how to apply it.

In Figure 14, you'll see a new hire example that includes multimedia orientation, web-based prework, classroom events with web-based simulations, games, tests, performance support, and an ongoing mentorship program that is at least partially managed by the learning function.

In this way, a model learner can be constructed so that we understand what learning and tool usage is mapped to improved performance. Not only can this inform the best designs for our learning environments, but it can also describe how best to engage with and use these resources to extract the best performance from people. For the first time, we have a fairly nonintrusive methodology for following the learner back to the job to monitor progress and understand what has worked well or not in terms of our learning and performance support offerings. This provides unprecedented insight into the relationship between learning and business performance.

Figure 14: NEW HIRE EXAMPLE

S U C C E S S ↑	**Performance on the job**	FPSS, Multimedia, Social Network, Performance Data, EMS, CRM
	Performance support/ Informal learning	EPSS, Multimedia, Social Network, WBT, EMS
	Classroom	Multimedia, EPSS, Games, Simulations, Social Network, LMS, EMS
	Prework	WBT, LMS, Multimedia, Games, Social Network, EMS
	Orientation	Multimedia, Social Network, EMS

As learners move through the learning landscape, various interactions result in usage data that can be mined and analyzed to create an electronic blueprint of usage. This blueprint can be compared with learning assessments and performance assessments after the learning events. The real value here is in combining the learning assessment data with ongoing performance support tool data as well as performance data to map typical usage and engagement behaviors to performance.

Figure 15: PERSONA

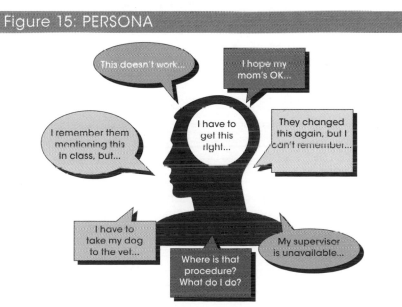

Data Sources and Analysis

Let's take a look at some data sources that can be found in most organizations, and briefly discuss some ways that this data can be leveraged for insight into the relationship between learning and business performance.

Orientation

Video and web-based training are great ways to orient new hires to the company. As people interact with these tools, usage data is collected by the multimedia server and LMS, that can be analyzed to understand full compliance as to whether all new hires watched the entire presentation, how long they spent on different sections, and whether they reviewed certain sections multiple times. This provides insight into interest level, which helps us to understand the value of the information or how to improve engagement. What may be considered important information to high-level leaders could potentially fall on uninterested ears, and it is typical that what people consider valuable will differ depending on the dynamics of the individual's demographics. What may be of value to someone hired as a business consultant could very well be quite different from that of someone hired into a customer-service position in a call center. We often make assumptions about what is interesting, so understanding the usage of an orientation piece and comparing that with various demographics could provide valuable insights into how to best orient a new employee into the job or into the company.

Web-Based Prework

This is an area that can be flubbed over by new hires or existing employees new to a particular job or role, but it represents a great approach to cost-effectively orient someone to the deeper learning that the classroom will provide. However, if people don't do the prework, they are behind from the start, which will detract from the deep learning of the classroom or more advanced online courses because the individual lacks the required basics and context. This is complicated by the fact that often a new hire's manager does not provide the individual with sufficient time to do the prework. Data analysis on who did the prework in an engaged fashion can be compared with those who did not or who were not engaged. This can help the learning leaders impress upon the business the value of the prework to obtain the proper buy-in. The usage data provides insight into how to create more engaging, more easily consumed prework, resulting in better classroom performance and better performance after class.

Classroom

Aside from tests and exit surveys, the classroom has little data-capture to understand individual or aggregate value. While these metrics have a long history, they do little to map the effectiveness of training to business performance. With big data, this is blown into many different advantageous analytic components. It's simply up to us to understand how to leverage these insights. Now we have the advantage of web based simulations, in-class use of EPSS as authoritative content, games, and the traditional test. In this scenario, all user performance data from all systems are analyzed and aggregated to determine what works best in planning learning events in addition to identifying certain types of learners and users that would benefit from different approaches. Adjustments can be made and then tested to determine if there are improvements in learning performance. This is then carried out through EPSS, performance analysis, and customer relationship management systems once the individual is out of training and on the job.

Performance Support

Performance support has a promising future as the backbone of the learning function and, to that end, usage data analysis becomes invaluable information in understanding the overall health of the learning function and associated resources. Through our research, we've determined that EPSS offer some of the most effective data available to understand what should drive the contents and contexts of the learning function. Due to the nature of its web-based content management technology, EPSS sits strategically between formal and informal learning. It is the authoritative source when a consensus cannot be reached. It is a bank of authoritative advice when there is uncertainty. It is vastly different than the classroom, web-based training, game, or multimedia experience intended to impress with storytelling. It is authoritative information available to people who have the appropriate decision-making context largely gained through formal learning experiences and on-the-job experience.

Data accumulated through the orientation, preclass, and classroom events can be analyzed relative to demographic data analysis, as well as EPSS usage. The data in aggregate can assist in building learner and EPSS profiles to understand what is truly valuable on the job relative to what learners were presented in formal learning environments. As a result, adjustments can be made to the classroom or to the performance support as different types of content benefit from different modalities.

Other Sources of Data

Aside from new opportunities for acquiring learner usage and performance data, there are other important sources that should be considered to compare and contrast the learning data and performance data. This information is important in developing personas, and is comparable to business intelligence and competitor intelligence in other business contexts, where data is heavily relied upon to improve business outcomes.

Demographic Data

Employee learning, performance, and customer relationship management systems are a wealth of useful information for better understanding learners' needs and the variables that affect or potentially predict future performance. It is a cornerstone of design that the designer must understand the intended end usage and end user in order to design an interaction the end user finds truly supportive, logical, and pleasant. Demographic data such as prior work experience, organizational position, geographic location, tenure within a particular role, previous education, prior training, prior learning performance, level of learning engagement, progress through the training program, previous success, previous performance issues, and so on, are invaluable for understanding how to make sense of the data accumulated through interactions with various systems. This is the humanizing data that provides context to the analytic data acquired through interactions with the learning and performance support systems. The value is in providing the human aspect to the human-system interactions. Until we get a handle on these interactions, we'll continue to struggle with providing people the right level of support.

Games

While the value of games for learning is a topic of debate, they are another source of data that can be useful in understanding learners and in assessing the effectiveness of the learning. The assumption here is that the value of games is not in their teaching function, but in their data-accumulation function. To that end, we're treating game performance as an assessment of the learning events and not necessarily a methodology for teaching material.

By treating data collection of game play similarly to the data collection of LMS, EPSS, multimedia, and performance management data, it becomes obvious that we gain understanding of an individual's performance within a designed environment through data that is created and tracked as an individual performs in the game. This is a "two-for-one," as the data can be used to assess an individual's understanding of the topic, as well as an ongoing assessment of the value of the learning event and tools.

An additional expected value of game analysis is in the capture of concepts, approaches, methodologies, and content for work that is more conceptual, investigative, or decision-oriented within a context of numerous moving parts and randomly incomplete information. For example, developing learning and support for a criminal investigator, or surgeon for that matter, is quite difficult because it depends on so many contextual factors. These factors can be identified and presented within the context of a game environment. By having experienced high-performers work through the games, data captured on the back end can track decisions made at crucial points. This data, in conjunction with anecdotal information through interviews and focus groups, can assist in the improved design of learning experiences.

Social Media

What treatise on big learning data could be complete without discussing the impact of social media? This technology is having an emerging effect on corporate and adult learning, but it's an important one as, historically, learning has been a social phenomenon, whether a group discussion, a pleasant chat over coffee, a team roundtable, or an after-action review. Social media is connecting experts to experts and laypersons alike. As these technologies are integrated into the learning function, social network analysis (SNA) should also be integrated. SNA is quite complex mathematically, but the statistical concepts are relatively simple and revolutionary in predictive analysis in concert with the statistical opportunities previously outlined. For example, through search-term analysis in EPSS, websites, and social network sites, it is possible to see, real-time, what the hot topics of the moment are. The learning professional can then assess the strength of their resources relative to what questions are out there. Maybe it is a new product or service, so there are few resources available. Without knowing that performers are in need of information, the learning professional is missing key information to improve these assets. In a way it's like magic, as the need can be identified near-real-time and the resource can be optimized quickly, leaving the performer to think, "Hey, I just had this problem Tuesday." This is getting us closer to seamless support and unparalleled performance.

What We Are Learning

Look at Things From Different Angles

Big data is random by nature, requiring an analytical approach to cut through it. However, when we begin to work through things analytically, we tend to do so from a predefined paradigm with predefined outcomes. This mindset doesn't work so well when it comes to the statistical analysis of large data sets. Data triggers occur as a user maneuvers through each interaction with an environment. This reality alone creates a tremendous amount of data, which pushes our resolve further and further to an intended outcome. But we have to remember that these data points represent human interactions, which can be aggregated and analyzed relative to established key performance indicators (KPIs) based on business goals and expected outcomes.

Using the game analytics example, each data-trigger node in Figure 16 represents a crucial decision to a goal which has been designed. If the goal is not successfully achieved, it is possible to determine where the mistake was made in the decision-making process—to see where the individual's understanding faltered. On the flip side, if the data indicate a significant percentage of people making the same mistake, there may be deficiencies in the learning or in the game itself.

Figure 16: GAME ANALYTICS EXAMPLE

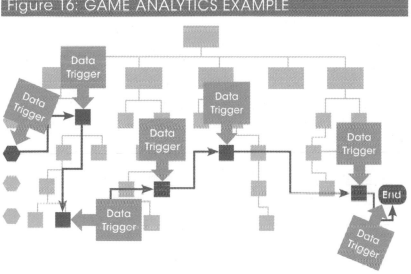

Design for Real People: Champions and Detractors

Too often, we, or our clients, make assumptions about what is important. Tools such as interviews, focus groups, and surveys help to obtain a sense of the learner, but each methodology is fraught with limitations and biases. To offset these biases and enrich our tool kit, I am exploring the use of personas. The persona is an important concept in e-commerce web analysis that is proving to be absolutely vital to understanding users and designing quality learning and support experiences. A *persona* is a model of a particular type of user. It is essentially a character with qualities of typical users based on certain types of demographics. A learning event, support tool, or multimedia resource can have many different personas, and a persona can require many different forms of support. So in essence, you are doubling the conceptual contexts that your data can shed light on. The nature of the persona is to identify how a particular type of user may need to engage in learning and support information.

There is no real limit to the number of personas that will be relevant to learning and support design, particularly as we realize the practice of learning-for-one, an à la carte future of self-directed learning. Typically, three to five personas per tool, event, or experience are sufficient to understand and capture the needs of the majority of learners. Yes, we are all very unique individuals; however, we're also very human and typically respond in rather predictable ways according to usual patterns. The persona helps us to understand what these patterns are relative to various demographic categories. The persona is why demographic and performance data that live outside of the learning environments are so important, as content can have a wide variety of users from high-level decision makers, to call center customer service reps, to new hires with an array of previous experiences and abilities. In addition, a persona must also take into account the various personal issues and point-in-life variations which all performers must balance relative to their work performance.

Persona analysis provides great insight into potential tool design and usage, as well as the content relative to different user groups. These are people who can help you understand how to refine the environment. This process can also assist in defining other important personas that may have not been recognized or kept in mind during the design phase. Examining usage behavior of both champions and detractors, thereby refining your persona profile, may uncover some behaviors or issues that could be mapped to actionable resolutions.

Design for Measurement

Each data stream has limitations in terms of what it can convey to cause and effect relationships, and it really means little until it is plugged into the proper algorithms.

Figure 17: BIG LEARNING DATA

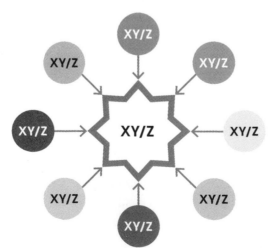

My biggest lightbulb moment was when I realized that you can't track and measure what hasn't been *designed* to be tracked and measured. Obviously, there are limits to this goal. Data analysis requires some key considerations to be made when designing experiences that will make the analytic process more manageable. Every design should have a clearly defined business goal. If a design element cannot be mapped back to a specified business outcome, then its value should be questioned.

Plugging this data into analytics to leverage the array of data streams available to us will result in a more sophisticated analysis that builds a more complete picture of the performance of our learning and support tools, as well as the needs of the performers themselves—and their actual performance. This analysis now shows a holistic view of all aspects of the experience, and we can drill down to assess across multiple variables. It is expected that we will have many ways to compare performance data against variables that we can control and manipulate in order to flesh out and fine tune learning and support in ways that move us much closer to learning-for-one.

To this end, one of the most useful tools is the "conversion funnel," a well-understood concept in e-commerce web analytics.

Figure 18: THE CONVERSION FUNNEL

Essentially, each goal—let's say video—should have an ideal path by which the user can navigate to it. These designs should account for navigation from a homepage, landing page, menu, or search results page, to properly capture various ways different users prefer to engage with information. This is at the heart of designing an environment to be measured, or, conversely, diagramming the best paths-to-access based on what you want to be measured. In this way, you can be sure that what you are measuring represents reliable usage data. As a result, significant effort, thought, research, and experimentation should be put into the navigation design from all user entry points, and it should be done outside of a client-sponsored project.

Don't Waste Your Time

One of the immediate impressions one has when working with large sets of various data sources is a sense of being completely and utterly overwhelmed. Well-established KPIs grounded in established business goals will help immensely with managing the overload of the amount of the data to parse and the typical noise to be found. Even then, it is easy to become enamored of the possibilities and lose sight of the purpose of exploring the data in the first place. To offset this, establish a few high-level indicators that will provide a snapshot of the health of a resource to help you focus your attention where you should: on issues that matter and that can be resolved. Currently, I am exploring the use of three KPIs that are simple to use, obtain, and understand, which I think will serve these purposes. The nice thing about them is how closely related they are, so that they serve as a sort of checks and balances against one another. These metrics provide a built-in cross-check for the analysis, while plugging them into various equations provides additional insights from which to hypothesize about issues, further research, and solutions. I call them the "health indicator trinity": recency, frequency, and friction.

Recency and frequency are important concepts in e-commerce web analysis, as they are based on a simple human psychological factor that the more recent and the more frequent someone has interacted with your service, and has been pleased with it, the more likely she is to interact with your service again. It is the single best predictor of whether people find the environment helpful. If it is helpful, they'll come back frequently, and often in relatively small time increments. Obviously, this does not apply carte blanche to all learning content or resources, as some are not intended to be referenced again and again. This emphasizes the importance of mapping your measurement strategy to your business strategy, and establishing proper baselines and thresholds for the intended usage, as well as assessing these metrics relative to the threshold set for the resource. However, once these baselines and thresholds are established, this metric is important to monitor as an indication that the resource is supporting or is not supporting people as intended.

Aside from the high-level health indices, recency and frequency can help us to differentiate user pools for further investigation. For example, personas, combined with recency and frequency, allow us to identify users who can provide valuable insights into the effectiveness of the learning and support environments. Users identified according to a particular persona with low recency and frequency rates can be interviewed about their usage of a tool, their confidence in it, their relative need for the resource, and their level of detraction. Users identified according to a particular persona with high recency and frequency rates can be interviewed regarding their usage along the same targets. These are our power users: Those who will promote the use of the tool and its effectiveness.

Friction is one of the most important indicators of the effectiveness of a tool. Metrically, friction can be grasped by understanding the recency and frequency baselines of the tool and its various users, as well as understanding the general latency of the resource and its users in aggregate. Conceptually, recency, frequency, and friction are tied together, with recency and frequency being metrical indicators of overall friction of a site. Once recency and frequency are established, they can be used to develop a friction indicator by looking at the percentage of people who do not fall within the established baseline of recency and frequency. A certain amount of friction is to be expected, so proper thresholds should be set for the friction you are willing to have relative to the recency and frequency behaviors of users in general. With time and effort, it is possible to become quite granular with this analysis in terms of mapping various demographic information about users to the results of these metrics. There is no other indicator as powerful as friction in signaling the need to redesign an experience or refresh the content.

A much simpler way of assessing friction is through "ping-ponging," a behavior easily identified in the usage data. Ping-ponging can be seen by a significant threshold of users clicking from one page to another and then back again repeatedly. This is typically seen on a homepage or landing page, but it can also happen along the conversion funnel path and search. Ping-ponging will typically lead to using the search page, which can also experience ping-ponging. The worst-case scenario here is that the user leaves the resource, which is known as fallout or leakage, and is also a clear indicator of a resource with a high level of friction. A deeper understanding of the issue is required to stop or diminish the leakage. Typically the issue is related to labeling, irrelevant content, visual design, or navigation design.

Drill Down by Going From Simple to Complex

Once you determine where to spend your time, suit up for the deep and the wide. This is where analysis becomes investigation, and by now you should have a good business case for engaging other data sets such as on-the-job performance data, individual demographic data, individual's learning experiences, interviews, focus groups, research, help desk log files, and so on, to create more sophisticated metrics. An example would be the latency index.

Latency is a more complex metric and is derived from recency, frequency, and friction metrics, as well as the dynamics of identified personas. It also provides a sense of keeping the data under control through increasingly complex statistical formulas. Latency has tremendous potential for learning because it adds an additional dynamic to understanding learners. It can be mapped to certain generic demographic information (personas) to set a standard of usage and performance based on variables such as tenure, learning experience (in the event of redesigns), work environment (comparing performance across teams and geography), and previous work experience. The basic premise is that it establishes a baseline of interactivity with a resource so that when a divergence is seen, it can be leveraged to determine whether the struggling individual is taking advantage of all of the tools, learning events, and support options as compared with those who perform well. And those who perform well, what do they do?

Latency establishes a pattern of expected interaction with an environment so that people struggling may be identified as outliers to the norm, based on the persona profiles that have been established for preferred performers. Significant deviation from this norm can identify performers at risk, or can be a check to determine how poor performers may be able to improve performance relative to the expectations of preferred performers. This norm is contingent on various demographic variables that allow us to slice and dice the information relative to these variables.

Conclusion

While we still have much to explore and learn about the impact of big learning data, one could argue that it can be a watershed for the potential to map the learning function to a clear return-on-investment. Return-on-investment has always been just out of reach for the learning field. Through some of the concepts, methodologies, and data sources discussed in this chapter, I am confident that it is possible to map the learning function directly to performance in ways previously unavailable. As we develop better strategies, resources, and tools for acquiring, aggregating, and analyzing data, not only will we create and optimize experiences, resources, and tools to support performers, we'll also be able to clearly define the contribution of learning to the bottom-line success of businesses.

CHAPTER 13

A PERSPECTIVE FROM K–12

A VIEW FROM THE U.S. DEPARTMENT OF EDUCATION ON BIG LEARNING DATA IN K–12

In addition to the perspectives shared by the contributors of this book, we also wanted to highlight what we see as some emerging trends in the kindergarten to high school (K-12) learning space. The U.S. Department of Education's Office of Educational Technology recently published its comprehensive report on the future of big learning data in this space. While the report is wide-ranging, we've highlighted key questions it addresses that we believe are relevant to our T&D world. In reviewing these questions, we see how the Department of Education is bringing focus to five primary areas for future work on big learning data in K-12: quality of innovation, adaptive learning, learner engagement, learning assessment, and decision making related to the adoption of learning resources.

Here are six questions posted by the U.S. Department of Education in their research: **How can education decision makers obtain the increased quality and quantity of evidence needed to fuel innovation and optimize the effectiveness of new technology-based learning resources?** Specifically, it identifies the increasing opportunities for technology and discusses the resulting need to leverage data and gather evidence to ensure better learning resources that promote deeper learning, develop adaptive learning systems that enable personalization, address sources of learning disengagement, improve learning assessment, and foster informed decisions about capitalizing on the explosion of learning resources. While the report focuses on K–12 education, the questions it addresses are also relevant in our organizational learning space.

"What can be done to ensure that technology-based resources and innovations are up to the task?"

The report opens with the challenge of promoting deeper learning, defined by the Hewlett Foundation as "the ability to acquire, apply, and expand academic content knowledge and to think critically about solving complex problems, communicating effectively, working collaboratively, and learning how to learn" (p. 12). The report asserts "technology advances hold great potential for educational outcomes and that evidence is what separates real advances from mere novelties" (p. vii). Emerging technologies make it possible to accomplish this through the more personalized approaches that they offer while capturing "micro-data" about learner interactions. Building new evidence making use of such data and analysis, therefore, will be key to determining whether these technologies are up to the task. Primary evidence-building approaches involve data mining, A/B comparison testing, and implementation research (assessing risk).

"How can the learning data these systems collect be used to improve the system's ability to adapt to different learners as they learn?"

The report highlights an emerging area for learning data: adaptive learning systems that "can support both the development and implementation of customized learning strategies and content for individual learners, including the ability to adapt to individual learners, as they use digital learning systems" (p. 35). These systems base adaptations not just on whether a student responds correctly or incorrectly, but also on a model of the student's thinking compared with a target knowledge model with goals to close the gap. Systems then update assumptions as students work through problems. This has implications for big data in matching learners with instructional approaches and developing expert learner models. Adaptive systems can also acquire "interests" data and adapt to the interests of students.

"How can data better be used to help support the full range of student needs and interests—both inside and outside schools and classrooms—to improve learning outcomes?"

The report addresses the topic of learning disengagement that impairs how students achieve learning progress, by leveraging data to support students and so reduce their disengagement. Sources of disengagement vary among learners, but the report postulates that use of big data can help. Technologies afford opportunities on various fronts, from leveraging predictive analytics that include nonlearning data, to better understanding the stressors that might affect learning, to digital badges that take into account the broader range of learning experience. Improved and linked data systems would support these technologies. The data and evidence challenge is in identifying and collecting relevant data about the learner and in validating the effectiveness of predictive models.

"How can educators use the system to measure more of what matters in ways that are useful for instruction?"

The report also focuses on improving the content and process of assessment with technology systems. An approach involves using online learning systems to collect (and analyze) more fine-grained information about student learning, such as: how quickly a student moves through a simulated environment or a sequence of problems; the amount of scaffolding and support the student needs; and changes in the student's response time across problems. This involves the shift for collecting assessment data after the learning to mining the data produced during the student interaction. In this approach, time does not have to be taken away from instruction to stop and measure how much was learned. Furthermore, this approach assesses over time and is not based on a discrete test at one moment in time. Evidence is still needed to understand the extent analytics effectively predict what students will do in other contexts, as well as to understand the impact of providing the learner feedback at the same time as assessments.

"What better support do educators need as they make decisions about which digital learning resources to adopt?"

The report also addresses the challenge of making informed choices as the range of options for content and resources grows. A technology-enabled approach—such as online repositories and communities that provide tailored assemblages of content—allows users to search curated collections of materials, upload and share their own materials, read and write reviews, create "playlists" of favorite resources, and interact with other users. They use Internet-supported techniques to help users find resources that might meet their needs. Questions remain on the effectiveness of specific resources along numerous criteria: design, fit, implementation, cost, time, and effectiveness in specific settings. This is prompting technology developers, companies, government entities, and nonprofit organizations to publish evidence about these issues. Their methods include aggregating user actions, aggregating user reviews, user panels, expert ratings and reviews, curation, and test beds.

The report concluded with a series of 14 roles-based recommendations. These roles recommend advancing the use of emerging technologies and providing necessary evidence to make sound decisions about which ones to use. These recommendations address relevant needs for the organizational workspace, including

* Collaborating to define problems of practice that can be addressed through digital learning and the associated kinds of evidence that can be collected to measure and inform progress in addressing these problems.

* Promoting education research designs that investigate whether and how digital learning resources teach aspects of deeper learning such as complex problem solving and promote the transfer of learning from one context to many contexts.

* Identifying the attributes of digital learning systems and resources that make a difference in learning outcomes.

References

U.S. Department of Education/Office of Educational Technology. (2013). *Expanding Evidence Approaches for Learning in a Digital World*. Retrieved on September 6, 2013 from www.ed.gov/edblogs/technology/files/2013/02/Expanding-Evidence-Approaches.pdf.

We encourage our readers to reference the U.S. Department of Education report at www.biglearningdata.com.

EPILOGUE

MOVING FORWARD

Bob Baker

So, how do we begin moving forward with big learning data? To address this, let's return to what Elliott Masie said in chapter 1: "Our hope is that you will be active learners, evidence-based experimenters, and explorers of both the opportunities and challenges that big learning data presents to the learning and knowledge world." As a Chief Learning Officer, I believe that we should consider how we leverage the perspectives provided in this book as learners, experimenters, and explorers. We should start asking and answering some important questions on behalf of our organizations and employees about the future of big learning data.

* **What makes big learning data and data analysis important for our organizations?** This is an important place to start, as we'll want to **focus** our learning, experiments, and explorations where they are most needed. It is apparent that private and public sector enterprises alike are increasing accountability on the learning function to affect performance, while opportunities are emerging for how big learning data and analysis can inform key areas such as: learning designs, investments, innovation, design, and a greater personalization of learning.

* **What does big learning data mean for learning personalization?** Clearly, the exciting thing about big learning data is that it creates the opportunity for a **shift** to personalized resources for our learners. This book highlights the potential that increasingly available big sets of data can help us to better understand, for example, learner interactions with learning content, as never before. With rich sets of data we also have the opportunity to develop scoreboards that help learners plan their learning activities. I really like the idea of scoreboards to help the learner make good learning choices that support the autonomy they will have with increased personalization.

* **How might big learning data play a key role in the life cycle of learning programs?** Increasingly, we will be able to **rethink** the data we use and move away from "silly data" to incorporate robust data approaches from inception to sustainment of learning programs. To do this, we will be challenged to move beyond well-ingrained mindsets about data and how we use it. The idea of starting small has an appeal. With that in mind, maybe there is a particular program, say new employee orientation, that opens the door to begin rethinking processes.

* **How does your organization grow and borrow the skills and mindsets to leverage big learning data?** We have a long way to go in our field to **grow** big data capabilities. This is obviously foundational to a big learning data approach and there are various options on how to develop this capacity both internally and externally as we determine the specific skill sets required. Let's consider acquiring skills for the short term to support early experiments, while considering a long-term approach that might involve a mix of developing skills within the learning function and external resources—either within or outside the organization.

* **How will the roles of learning leaders need to evolve to foster a big learning data approach in our organizations?** One key takeaway from this book is that to begin moving forward with big learning data, learning leader roles will need to **evolve**. It is not too early to consider the emerging roles and relationships that will be required to develop a big learning data approach. Start

with important steps: building relationships with key data sources outside the learning enterprise and stakeholders that will both provide and benofit from big learning data; guarding against the traps that are inherent in this approach; and keeping alert to the honest and challenging conversations organizations should have about the risks associated with a big learning data approach.

Each organization will have a unique context, need, and capacity to address these questions—and others that you might come up with. Move forward—as learners, experimenters, and explorers—creating and shaping big learning data to create big, personalized, and effective learning for employees and organizations!

ABOUT THE AUTHORS

Elliott Masie
President, CEO, and Founder
The MASIE Center

Elliott Masie is a provocative, engaging, and entertaining futurist, analyst, and speaker. He enjoys topics related to learning, technology, data, and workplace performance. Elliott has varied feelings about big data; he is simultaneously intrigued, challenged, excited, and concerned about how big data will be experienced by employees, citizens, and organizations.

Elliott is the editor of Learning TRENDS by Elliott Masie, an Internet newsletter read by more than 52,000 business executives worldwide, and is a regular columnist in several publications. He hosts an annual learning conference each fall, bringing together thousands of learning professionals to benchmark and collaborate on the rapidly changing world of learning and workplace performance.

For almost four decades, Elliott's focus has been the evolution of learning, including the use of technology for knowledge, learning, and collaboration throughout organizations. Elliott is acknowledged as the first analyst to use the term "e-learning" in the 1990s, and he has been on the forefront of social, mobile, and video-based learning experiments.

Elliott serves as an advisor to a wide range of government, education, and nonprofit groups. His board service has included the Board of Trustees of Skidmore College, FIRST Robotics Board of Directors, and several venture startups. He served on the CIA University Board of Visitors and the White House Advisory Council on Expanding Learning Opportunities.

Throughout his career, Elliott has been fascinated by data and the analysis of human and organizational behaviors. His work with the intelligence community has provided a context for the future of really big data and how technology can harvest an almost unimaginable degree of data points—some providing real context, and others pure data exhaust. Elliott is facilitating a set of high-level dialogues with industry, government, and association leaders on bringing transparency, overtness, and citizen choice to the big data conversations.

He lives in Saratoga Springs, owns thoroughbred horses, and is a producer/investor in Broadway shows, including the Tony Award-winning *Kinky Boots, A Time to Kill,* and *The Trip to Bountiful,* as well as *Macbeth, Allegiance,* and *Somewhere in Time.* His email is emasie@masie.com and you can find his work at www.masie.com.

masie The MASIE Center
Learning CONSORTIUM The MASIE Center is a Saratoga Springs, NY, think-tank focused on how organizations can support learning and knowledge within the workforce. The center hosts the Learning CONSORTIUM: a coalition of more than 200 global organizations cooperating on the evolution of learning strategies. Member organizations include CNN, Walmart, American Express, Southwest Airlines, Farmers Insurance, Emirates Airline, Starbucks, General Electric, and Fidelity Investments.

Bob Baker
Chief Learning Officer
The MASIE Center

Bob Baker is the Chief Learning Officer at the MASIE Center and Learning CONSORTIUM. He works with members to provide thought leadership in workplace learning. For example, he has recently supported MASIE Learning CONSORTIUM projects and learning labs focused on emerging technologies, curating social learning, e-books, the future classroom, the virtual classroom, technical training, video for learning, and learning strategy.

He served in the Central Intelligence Agency for more than 31 years, most recently as the deputy and acting Chief Learning Officer, prior to joining the MASIE Center in June 2011.

Nigel Paine
Managing Director
nigelpaine.com ltd.

Nigel Paine has been involved in corporate learning for more than 20 years. He has run organizations producing learning software, CDs, and multimedia materials, and has offered learning resources to companies large and small. Appointed in April 2002 to head up the BBC's training and development operation, he built a successful training and development operation which included state of the art informal learning and knowledge sharing.

He left the BBC in September 2006 to start his own company focused on building great workplaces by promoting creativity, innovation, and learning, and the link between them. He speaks at conferences around the world and writes for a range of international publications. He is also coaching senior executives in companies in Europe, Australia, and the United States. He is currently writing a book on the challenges of 21st century learning leadership.

Donald H. Taylor
Chairman
Learning and Performance Institute

Donald H. Taylor is a 25-year veteran of the learning, skills, and human capital industries, with experience at every level from design and delivery to chairman of the board. He has been chairman of the Learning and Performance Institute since 2010. A recognized commentator and organizer in the fields of workplace learning and learning technologies, he is passionately committed to helping develop the training and development profession.

His background ranges from training delivery to director and vice-president positions in software companies. He has been a company director and shareholder for three companies through startup, growth, and acquisition. He is an influential writer and speaker in the fields of the professional development of T&D and of technology-supported learning.

Tom King
Chief Learning Technologist
Boeing Flight Services

Tom King is chief learning technologist of Boeing Flight Services, which provides innovative flight and maintenance training products and services for commercial airline pilots, technicians, and flight crews. He leads a team responsible for enhancing the user experience and creating innovative solutions for all forms of e-learning and technology-assisted instruction available across the curriculum.

Before joining Boeing Flight Services in 2010, he held positions with Macromedia/Adobe, Authorware Inc., Andersen Consulting, Lotus/IBM Learning Services, and Questionmark Corp. He has been actively involved with many e-learning technology specification groups, including ADL SCORM, AICC, IEEE LTSC, and others. He has a master's degree in instructional design and more than 20 years of experience developing and managing e-learning materials.

Coley O'Brien
Vice President of HR and Field Capability
The Wendy's Company

Coley leads the field operations and corporate training function for Wendy's, supporting nearly 250,000 crew members, managers, and multi-unit operators in 6,600 company and franchise restaurants. He has more than 15 years of progressive experience in corporate learning functions and consulting, including positions with Sears, Thomson NETg, and Arthur Andersen. In these roles, he has helped architect and implement broad-based learning strategies comprised of blended learning solutions, traditional e-learning, performance-support tools, custom business simulations, and instructor-led offerings.

He has presented at numerous learning conferences and participates on multiple customer advisory boards with vendors in the learning space. He has a master's degree in instructional systems technology from the University of Indiana.

Rahul Varma
Chief Learning Officer
Accenture

Rahul is Accenture's Chief Learning Officer and is a member of Accenture's Human Resources Executive Leadership Team. Accenture invests more than $850 million in training, and as the Chief Learning Officer, Rahul is responsible for defining Accenture's overall learning strategy; design and delivery of all learning programs for Accenture's more than 266,000 employees; and ensuring that they have the right skills to support client needs and growth of Accenture.

Prior to his current role, Rahul was the global HR Strategy Director and also led the implementation of Accenture's HR Transformation program. He started his career with Accenture in India and served as the first India HR Director leading HR through a period of significant growth in the country.

Dan Bielenberg
Director of Capability Development
Strategy
Accenture

Dan leads the capability development strategy team for Accenture's global Center of Expertise. He is responsible for overall learning strategy and learning architectures for Accenture. Dan has 25 years of experience in organizational learning, from strategy formulation to instructional design and technology innovation.

His current focus is developing strategies and solutions to address the critical talent challenges across Accenture's diverse global workforce. Dan has a master's degree in instructional systems design from Florida State University.

Dana Alan Koch
Learning Strategist
Accenture

In Dana Alan Koch's 25 years with Accenture, he has architected, designed, and developed hundreds of hours of computer-based, instructor-led, and mobile learning courses for global audiences. Currently, he defines new learning architectures and determines how to use new tools, technologies, and approaches to improve performance and learning at Accenture. He is also part of a team that is implementing human-centered design methods within Accenture to ensure Accenture keeps the human experience central to designs of its processes, learning, and systems.

He is a frequent presenter at international conferences and has published articles on various learning-related topics, including mobile learning and high-performance learning. He has a BA from Brigham Young University in organizational communications, and an MA from Northwestern University in learning science and adult learning.

A.D. Detrick
Measurement Consultant
Intrepid Learning

A.D. has more than 15 years of experience in the strategy, design, and measurement of learning initiatives. Presently, A.D. designs measurement and business impact strategies for clients in a wide range of industries. With a background in psychometrics and data analysis, he has designed multiple systems to monitor training events, defined performance thresholds, and helped numerous T&D organizations align training efforts with the bottom line.

Prior to joining Intrepid, A.D. created and managed the entire learning measurement strategy for JPMorgan Chase's consumer banking division. He also served as the national training manager for CheckFree Corporation's Global Knowledge Management group, where he trained business analysts on data science. As a researcher and a presenter, A.D. is continually searching for ways to improve the validity and value of T&D to the organizations with whom he works.

Nickole Hansen
Director of Learning
Grant Thornton LLP

Nickole began her career in the hotel and restaurant industry, where she managed a restaurant and supported hotel sales and convention services. From there, she joined Grant Thornton as a meeting planner. During her time within the travel and procurement area, she facilitated the implementation and change management of a firm-wide travel booking platform, e-procurement system, and nationalized airline and hotel programs.

She then moved into learning organizations, where she has led the project management and change efforts in many large firm-wide learning technology implementations, including a learning management system, compliance reporting system, and webcasting platforms. She has managed several areas within the learning organization: program delivery, learning operations and resource management, and learning compliance. Most recently, Nickole is responsible for driving the strategy and change efforts for learning performance measurement and analytics and special projects. Nickole holds a BS from Iowa State University in hotel and restaurant management, and is a certified Project Management Professional (PMP).

Peggy Parskey
Strategic Measurement Consultant
KnowledgeAdvisors

Assistant Director
Center for Talent Reporting

Peggy has more than 25 years of experience in driving strategic change to improve organizational and individual performance. She draws upon varied disciplines, including change management, human performance improvement, and project management to set program goals, define success measures, and develop tactical plans. Her focus and passion over the past several years has been in the field of measurement and evaluation. In her role with KnowledgeAdvisors, she guides organizations in developing measurement strategies, aligning learning metrics with organizational goals, integrating evaluation into business and learning processes, conducting training business impact studies, and implementing executive reporting systems and processes.

In addition, she is the assistant director of the Center for Talent Reporting, which was launched in October 2012. In this role, she is responsible for the credentialing of talent practitioners in the execution of talent development reporting principles within their organizations or with clients. She has also authored several articles and whitepapers on measurement and management of change. She is certified in management of change methodologies. She holds a BS in mathematics from Simmons College and master's degrees from the University of Chicago in statistics and business administration.

Jennifer O'Brien
Director, Consulting
KnowledgeAdvisors

As a director on the consulting team, Jennifer serves as the lead consultant for several strategic accounts while managing a team of consultants. Jennifer has more than 13 years of experience both within and outside of KnowledgeAdvisors in improving organizational and individual performance. Her primary focus has been assisting organizations in developing measurement tools that demonstrate the effectiveness and value of their services. Jennifer works closely with organizations in developing measurement strategies; designing surveys; aligning learning metrics with organizational goals; and analyzing, communicating, and taking action on measurement data.

Jennifer has also helped many clients build dashboards for their measurement data through the use of technology and data-visualization techniques. Before KnowledgeAdvisors, Jennifer worked with nonprofit and government organizations to develop strategies to better measure the results their clients were achieving and then using that information to improve organizational programs.

Jeff Losey
Head of Professional Development Center
University of Farmers, Claims

Head of the University of Farmers, Claims' Professional Development Center since its 2012 founding, Jeff Losey brings extensive insurance management and staff development experience to his role. Before joining the University staff, he led the reorganization of Farmers' large property, commercial property, and catastrophe units, and delivered top-tier customer service and quality results every year in each department.

Losey began his Farmers career in 1986 as a claims representative, and moved through branch and zone leadership roles in multiple lines—including property, auto, liability, commercial, med/PIP, and subrogation—before becoming national manager of large property in 2000. He moved to a director role in commercial property in 2003, and was then named AVP of commercial, large property, and catastrophe in 2005 before becoming VP of property claims in 2009.

Ben Morrison
Training Project Consultant
Southwest Airlines

Ben Morrison has 19 years of training experience. He started in 1997 with one of the nation's largest drugstore retailers as a developer of point-of-sale training. He later designed computer-based training and eventually moved into leadership training. He joined Southwest in 2001 as an instructional designer for the University for People, which was geared toward developing leadership throughout Southwest Airlines.

Since then, Ben has spent time in inflight training, ground operations training, and reservations training. These training departments have now merged, which allowed him to take on his latest role as a training project consultant, where he focuses on improving training development and delivery processes as well as training evaluation.

Doug Armstrong
Analytic Consultant
Working with Progressive Insurance

Doug's academic background is in cognitive science, linguistics, and biology. For the last 13 years, he has worked in the electronic performance support arena as a developer, a manager of developers, and a strategist. During the last five years, his focus has been enhancing performance support by leveraging EPSS technologies, information archi lecture, enterprise content management, enterprise search management, taxonomies, and analytics.

His current interests relative to analytics are in leveraging various data streams to create performance management processes for learning systems, for support tool systems, and for performer support.

INDEX

A

A/B test, 33

Accenture, 20, 50

accountability case study, Grant Thornton

    background, 76–77

    current state of measurement, 80–81

    evaluation model, 78

    future plans, 81–82

    leadership buy-in, 77–78

    measurement strategy, developing a,

        78–80

actionable metrics versus vanity metrics,

    32–33

Advanced Qualification Program, FAA, 42

Amazon.com, 15, 18

analytical skills, need for, 24–26

B

Bassey, L., 17

Beane, B., 57

big data. *See* big learning data

big learning data

    See also data analytics; data mining

      mistakes; learning analytics

    challenges, 3–4, 13

    characteristics of, 2–3

    collection issues, 11–12

    defined, 3, 18

    determining valuable, 13

    future for, 15

    impact of, 1–2, 9–10, 14

    importance of, 17–20, 127

    key points, 20–21

    shifts needed, 12–13

    sources of, 10–12

Bilek, J., 95

Black Swan, The (Taleb), 58

Blank, S. G., 32

Boston Red Sox, 57–58

Bowman, D., 56

business results, 53

C

Capability Map, 24

catalyst, 47

Chudler, E., 25

Cisco, 1

collaboration, 71

connector, 46–47

consistency, 40

context expert, 48

conversion funnel, 117

course design

    actionable metrics versus vanity

      metrics, 32–33

    crowdsourcing, 37

    disparate data, working with, 38–39

    lean canvas design, 35–37

    lean startup, 32

HOW TO PURCHASE ASTD PRESS PRODUCTS

All ASTD Press titles may be purchased through ASTD's online store at **www.store.astd.org**.

ASTD Press products are available worldwide through various outlets and booksellers. In the United States and Canada, individuals may also purchase titles (print or eBook) from:

Amazon– www.amazon.com (USA); www.amazon.com (CA)
Google Play– play.google.com/store
EBSCO– www.ebscohost.com/ebooks/home

Outside the United States, English-language ASTD Press titles may be purchased through distributors (divided geographically).

**United Kingdom, Continental Europe,
the Middle East, North Africa, Central Asia,
and Latin America:**
Eurospan Group
Phone: 44.1767.604.972
Fax: 44.1767.601.640
Email: eurospan@turpin-distribution.com
Web: www.eurospanbookstore.com
For a complete list of countries serviced via Eurospan please visit www.store.astd.org or email publications@astd.org.

South Africa:
Knowledge Resources
Phone: +27(11)880-8540
Fax: +27(11)880-8700/9829
Email: mail@knowres.co.za
Web: http://www.kr.co.za
For a complete list of countries serviced via Knowledge Resources please visit www.store.astd.org or email publications@astd.org.

Nigeria:
Paradise Bookshops
Phone: 08033075133
Email: paradisebookshops@gmail.com
Website: www.paradisebookshops.com

Asia:
Cengage Learning Asia Pte. Ltd.
Email: asia.info@cengage.com
Web: www.cengageasia.com
For a complete list of countries serviced via Cengage Learning please visit www.store.astd.org or email publications@astd.org.

India:
Cengage India Pvt. Ltd.
Phone: 011 43644 1111
Fax: 011 4364 1100
Email: asia.infoindia@cengage.com

For all other countries, customers may send their publication orders directly to ASTD. Please visit: **www.store.astd.org**.